100 WALKS IN
YORKSHIRE

WEST RIDING & THE DALES

JONATHAN SMITH

THE CROWOOD PRESS

First published in 2015 by
The Crowood Press Ltd
Ramsbury, Marlborough
Wiltshire SN8 2HR

enquiries@crowood.com

www.crowood.com

This impression 2021

British Library Cataloguing-in-Publication Data
A catalogue record for this book is available from the British Library.

ISBN 978 1 84797 909 4

Mapping in this book is sourced from the following products: OS Explorer 278, 288, 297,
298, 299, 304, OL1, OL2, OL19, OL21, OL30, OL298 and OL302
© Crown copyright 2015 Ordnance Survey. Licence number 100038003

Every effort has been made to ensure the accuracy of this book. However, changes can
occur during the lifetime of an edition. The Publishers cannot be held responsible for any
errors or omissions or for the consequences of any reliance on the information given in
this book, but should be very grateful if walkers could let us know of any inaccuracies by
writing to us at the address above or via the website.

As with any outdoor activity, accidents and injury can occur. We strongly advise readers to
check the local weather forecast before setting out and to take an OS map. The Publishers
accept no responsibility for any injuries which may occur in relation to following the walk
descriptions contained within this book.

Graphic design and typesetting by Peggy & Co. Design Inc.
Printed and bound in India by Replika Press Pvt. Ltd.

Contents

How to Use this Book

The book is divided into two distinct parts: The Dales and West Riding. The walks in each of these sections are ordered by distance, starting with the shortest. An information panel for each walk shows the distance, start point (see below), a summary of route terrain and level of difficulty (Easy/Moderate/Difficult), OS map(s) required, and suggested pubs/cafés at the start/end of walk or *en route*.

Readers should be aware that starting point postcodes have been supplied for satnav purposes and are not indicative of exact locations. Some start points are so remote that there is no postcode.

Maps

There are 92 maps covering the 100 walks. Some of the walks are extensions of existing routes and the information panel for these walks will tell you the distance of the short and long versions of the walk. For those not wishing to undertake the longer versions of these walks, the 'short-cuts' are shown on the map in red.

The routes marked on the maps are punctuated by a series of numbered waypoints. These relate to the same numbers shown in the walk description.

Start Points

The start of each walk is given as a postcode and also a six-figure grid reference number prefixed by two letters (which indicates the relevant square on the National Grid). More information on grid references is found on Ordnance Survey maps.

Parking

Many of the car parks suggested are public, but for some walks you will have to park on the roadside or in a lay-by. Please be considerate when leaving your car and do not block access roads or gates. Also, if parking in a pub car park for the duration of the walk, please try to avoid busy times.

Countryside Code

- Consider the local community and other people enjoying the outdoors
- Leave gates and property as you find them and follow paths
- Leave no trace of your visit and take litter home
- Keep dogs under effective control
- Plan ahead and be prepared
- Follow advice and local signs

Walks Locator

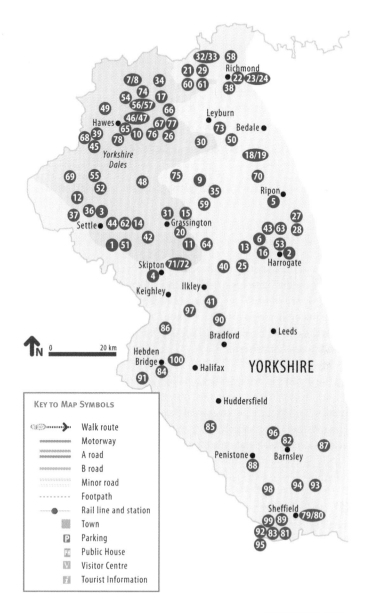

Seven Stiles from Long Preston

START The Green at Long Preston, BD23 4NJ, GR SD835582

DISTANCE 2½ miles (4km)

SUMMARY An easy, short walk along lanes and paths

MAPS OS Explorer OL2 Yorkshire Dales: Southern and Western Areas; OS Landranger 103 Blackburn & Burnley

WHERE TO EAT AND DRINK Long Preston has two pubs: the Maypole, T01729-840219, and the Boar's Head, T01729-840217

A straightforward walk with a lovely section of riverside and then good views towards Pendle Hill.

① From the Maypole Inn head east for 200yds until a school appears on the right. Just past the school turn right and follow the lane down towards an attractive fourteenth-century church. It is worth going in and having a look both at the church itself and the graveyard. From the church head along a lane east for 250yds until it dips and then crosses Long Preston Beck.

② Just past the bridge take a small style to the right and follow an intermittent path alongside the river. A barn is passed and soon two small stiles. To the right is a circular stone wall, which contains the Long Preston water supply. Keep to the riverside and pass across two fields – keep an eye out for rabbits in the hillside to the right. Another stile is passed as the path sticks close to the river for 100yds before opening up where the river divides.

③ The path you are after is on the hillside to the left, so cross two small bridges to get there – do not head up the track to the right.

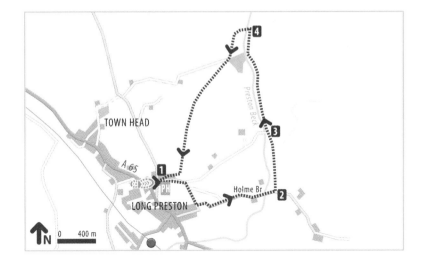

4 The path doubles back on itself and climbs towards a gate. Pass through it and a few yards further take the small gate through the wall directly ahead. This is the start of the seven stiles, so start counting. Walk south-west across the field, which has excellent views over Pendle, and aim for two trees. At the field boundary there is a small stile and from here Long Preston appears in view below. The path carries on south-west and crosses three more stiles (close together) before levelling out. The path, which may be difficult to follow, bends more to the west, and crosses two more stiles before emerging on a lane. Turn left and complete the final few yards back into Long Preston village.

Points of interest

 Set in a small copse, St Mary's Church has its origins in Norman times but also includes some lovely Georgian features and an exquisite seventeenth-century pulpit.

At the Maypole in Long Preston a true English tradition is enacted on the first Saturday in May, when the local schoolchildren dance around the maypole under the direction of a locally selected May Queen.

START The Valley Gardens, Harrogate, HG1 2SZ, GR SE293557

DISTANCE 3 miles (5km)

SUMMARY Easy along paths and lanes near the town centre

MAPS OS Explorer 297 Lower Wharfedale and Washburn Valley; OS Landranger 104 Leeds & Bradford

WHERE TO EAT AND DRINK
The Harrogate Arms Hotel, Crag La, T01423-567950;
Betty's, Parliament St, T0845-6001919, Yorkshire's most famous tearooms!

A tremendously varied short walk, going from the town centre to open countryside.

1 From Harrogate town centre enter the Valley Gardens through the main gates. Follow the left-hand path along the stream, recently named the 'Elgar Walk' to commemorate the composer's frequent visits to the town. At Bogs Field, site of no less than thirty-six different mineral springs, take the path that runs to the right of the tennis courts. On reaching the woods, take the second of two paths to your right, signposted 'Harlow Carr Gardens'.

2 Follow the path through the pinewoods to Harlow Moor Rd. Cross this road, and a few yards to the left follow a path signposted 'Crag Lane, Harlow Carr Gardens'. Indistinct at first, this path goes through woodland and then passes along the right-hand edge of a grassy clearing to join a metalled path.

3 As this path reaches Crag La, Harlow Carr Botanical Gardens is in front of you. If you wish to visit the gardens, the entrance is 50yds to the left; otherwise follow the road to your right.

4 The road soon becomes a stony path and eventually veers right. After about 10yds follow the footpath sign to the left, marked 'Cornwall Road'. You are now at the top of Birk Crag. Ahead, across the valley, is Queen Ethelburga's School, and slightly to the left is the Army Apprentice's College with its unusual pyramid-shaped chapels.

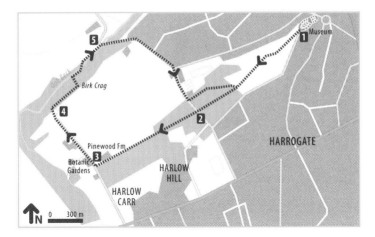

The path follows the top of the crag and then falls steeply in a series of rough steps. Follow these to the left. After the first set of steps, ignore the path directly ahead and turn sharp left down a further flight. At the foot of the steps the path begins to rise slightly, and runs parallel with Oak Beck. After approximately 100yds take the rough wooden steps to your left down to the beck, and then continue right along the bank to the bridge on Cornwall Rd.

⑤   Turn right and follow the road until you see the pinewoods to your left. The first path through them will take you back into the Valley Gardens.

Points of interest

Harrogate is famous for its beautiful gardens, elegant Victorian architecture and fine conference and shopping facilities. At the Pump Room Museum, close to the entrance to the Valley Gardens, you can discover Harrogate's past and taste the waters which brought fame and prosperity to the town. The Valley Gardens are taken over for a few days in spring by the annual flower shows. The Tourist Information Centre will have the dates.

Harlow Carr Botanical Gardens – beautiful surroundings in which to learn more about the art of gardening or simply to enjoy a relaxing stroll. As well as showcasing a variety of gardens, Harlow Carr contains an alpine house, arboretum and woodland walks with stunning displays of rhododendrons.

Stainforth Waterfalls

START The car park at Stainforth, just off the B6479, BD24 9PB, GR SD821674 (the car park is just to the south-west of the market place; cross the market past the Co-op to start the walk)

DISTANCE 3 miles (5km)

SUMMARY Easy

MAPS OS Explorer OL2 Yorkshire Dales: Southern and Western Areas; OS Landranger 98 Wensleydale & Upper Wharfedale

WHERE TO EAT AND DRINK Stainforth is a small village with a worthy pub, the Craven Heifer (T01729-822599), which caters for walkers with good beer, food and welcomes dogs and all-comers

A short, easy walk, steep in places, to two waterfalls and a historic packhorse bridge.

[1] From Stainforth, turn right out of the car park and left along the road signposted 'Halton Gill'. Go over the green on your right, cross Stainforth Beck via the stepping stones, then bear left up a stony lane. At the top of this lane go left down a steep hill to Catrigg Force. Take care as the hill can be slippery when it is wet and you come upon the force very suddenly.

[2] Return to the lane. The views from here are splendid, with Pen-y-Ghent ahead of you as you face Catrigg, and Fountains Fell to the right. Go over the stile at the end of the lane and turn left. Cross a further stile and follow the signpost to Winskill. When your path is crossed by another path, go through the gate marked Lower Winskill and down the lane. Pass the house and go through a yard to cross a ladder stile.

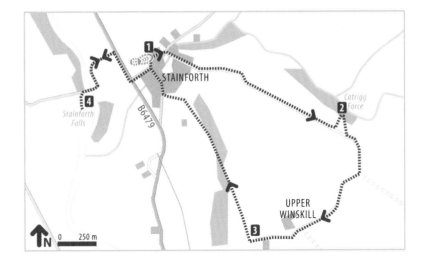

③ Follow the path, right, alongside the wall to cross a further stile and then go half left (the path is obscure here) over an area of exposed limestone. A further stile takes you into a small copse and then passes alongside a limestone scar. At the end of the scar go through the gap in the wall and take the leftmost fork of the path down to the road. Turn right over the bridge, left past the car park and right at the main road.

④ Take the first turning on the left over the railway bridge to reach the beautiful Packhorse Bridge at Little Stainforth. Just over the bridge a footpath to your left takes you to Stainforth Falls, idyllically set on a bend in the River Ribble. After visiting the falls, retrace your steps to the car park.

Points of interest

Stainforth derives its name from the 'stony ford' which linked the two settlements – Stainforth and Little Stainforth – on either side of the River Ribble. Once, it was on an important packhorse route between York and Lancaster.

The Packhorse Bridge at Little Stainforth is now owned by the National Trust. It was built in the 1670s.

Skipton

START Skipton main car park,
just off the market square,
BD23 1AH, GR SD991516

DISTANCE 3½ miles (5.5km)

SUMMARY Easy

MAPS OS Explorer OL2 Yorkshire
Dales: Southern and Western Areas;
OS Landranger 103 Blackburn & Burnley

WHERE TO EAT AND DRINK
The Craven Heifer Inn (T01756-792521)
and a variety of places in Skipton

A pleasant circular walk through Civil War country.

1 Walk onto the main street and turn right towards the parish church. From the church go left, along the Grassington road, passing the Castle Inn, crossing the canal and turning right up Chapel Hill. Where the road bifurcates, take the left fork, going uphill to enter a field over a stile beside a gate. Continue northwards up the field to exit over another stile beside a gate at the top. From this vantage point the views of Skipton and the Aire valley are excellent. Continue along the footpath ahead, going downhill to reach the busy Skipton by-pass road.

2 Cross the by-pass to a stile and go over into a field to the left of a golf course. Keeping in the same direction, cross the field to a stile on the brow of the hill ahead. Cross to reach the golf course. Continue straight ahead to the corner of two stone walls. There, go over a stone stile and on to a gate. Go through into a field. Cross the field, keeping close to its left-hand side, to reach another stile. Cross to reach Brackenly La to the north of Tarn Moor.

3 Turn left and go along it until you reach the main road from Skipton to Grassington. To the left of the T-junction stands the Craven Heifer Inn, which makes a handy mid-walk refreshment stop.

4 From the T-junction cross the road to the stile immediately opposite and go over to a field. Cross the field and exit at a stile opposite. Continue over the next field, aiming for an electricity pole, and keep in the same direction to reach a stile beside a gate. Cross to reach Bog La. Turn left along it.

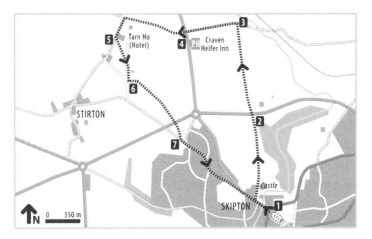

5 About 100yds after passing Tarn House Farm, go over a large stile on your left into a field. Cross the field, going between two large trees to an old kissing gate. Go through into a lane. Now turn right and follow waymarkers around the right side of a caravan park.

6 When a wooden stile is reached, cross it to enter a large field. Continue ahead, passing an electricity pole, to a tree on the horizon and, keeping it on your right, continue in the same direction to cross a broken stile onto a busy road. Cross the road and the stile immediately opposite into a field. Cross the road to reach the Skipton to Stirton road over another stile.

7 Turn left along it, and on reaching Skipton go downhill along Raikes Rd until you arrive at Skipton parish church – the end of a grand little walk.

Points of interest

The earthworks you cross on the hill approaching the by-pass were thrown up during the Civil War, when there was much local action. Arum lilies, violets, wood sorrel and many other plants grow in the hedgerow along Bog La.

Fountains Abbey & Studley Royal

START National Trust car park,
Fountains Abbey,
HG4 3DY, GR SE270682

DISTANCE 4 miles (6.5km)

SUMMARY Easy walking on
paths over relatively flat terrain

MAPS OS Explorer 299 Ripon
& Boroughbridge; OS Landranger
99 Northallerton & Ripon

WHERE TO EAT AND DRINK
National Trust tearooms at Fountains
Abbey towards the end of the walk

The walk skirts the Fountains Abbey estate with views of the abbey, and passes
through an eighteenth-century landscape garden.

1   Leave the car park and turn right up the hill, bearing left as the
road forks. After approximately 300yds take the footpath on the left.
As the path rises, the view of Fountains Abbey is particularly fine.
After a mile the path goes through a gate into a field. After 100yds the
path bends to the right, goes through another gate and then after a
further 50yds bends left towards Hill House Farm.

2   Turn left through a gate into the farm and immediately bend
right in front of the barns. Follow the markers left and then right and
through a gate. Take the track ahead for about 150yds, but where it
bends right go straight on, making for a gate into the woods ahead.
Follow the woodland path for about half a mile, emerging into a
clearing, and take the lower of the two tracks on the left, signposted to
Ripon.

3   After 200yds turn left at the stream and cross the bridge. Turn left
and after a further 200yds go through the gate into Studley Park. This
is a deer park, so dogs must be kept on leads. Follow the path, which
crosses the River Skell six times. After the sixth bridge (over the weir)
head uphill towards the church and obelisk.

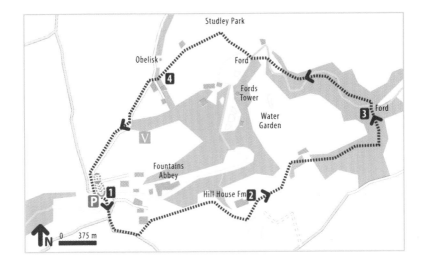

4️⃣   Take the path in front of the church to the left, and leave the park at the gate. Follow the road to a junction, then turn left along the main road as far as the gatehouse (now a gift shop). Go straight ahead if you wish to visit Fountains Abbey, otherwise turn right for the car park.

Points of interest

🔍   Fountains Abbey, now a World Heritage Site, was built in the twelfth century by Benedictine monks who had adopted the Cistercian rule. The extensive ruins are in a beautiful riverside setting and are one of the best preserved abbey ruins in the country.

Studley Park was created between 1716 and 1781. A formal water garden, deer park and various follies are incorporated into the natural landscape.

Hampsthwaite & Clint

START The village green,
Hampsthwaite, HG3 2BU, GR SE258587

DISTANCE 4 miles (6.5km)

SUMMARY Easy along lanes
and well marked paths

MAPS OS Explorer 298
Nidderdale; OS Landranger
99 Northallerton & Ripon

WHERE TO EAT AND DRINK Castle
Tea Rooms, Ripley, T01423-770152
(Tue–Sun, 12–6pm); The Nelson Inn
at Hampsthwaite, T01423-500340

An interesting walk with lots of history as you pass the grounds of Ripley castle,
and with views along the Nidd valley.

[1]   Walk towards Clint. Continue down the road, passing St Thomas
à Becket church, and go over the bridge to a sharp right-hand bend
in the road. The route goes straight ahead through a gate and climbs
up the steep hill with a hedge on the right. Do stop and enjoy the
splendid view into the valley of the Nidd. Go over stiles onto the road,
with the tiny hamlet of Clint to your left.

[2]   Turn right along the lane marked with a dead-end sign and
follow it for about half a mile to a gate leading into Hollybank Wood.
Meander through this lovely wood along the path over a bridge
spanning Ripley Beck. At this point you have a good view of Ripley
Castle and the lake. The way now takes you into the picturesque
cobbled square of this old market town.

[3]   Leave Ripley along the same path by which you entered the
village. Go down over the beck to a fork junction. Turn right and,
keeping the wall on your right, follow a track, passing Sadler Carr
Farm, Alicia Wood and Park Lodge all to the left.

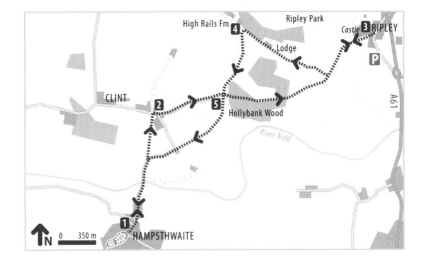

4. Before you come to High Rails Farm, there is a junction: go left through the gate and straight ahead over the fields on a well-defined bridle path, meeting up with the road where you entered Hollybank Wood.

5. Cross the road and go down the bridle path, linking up with the main road back to Hampsthwaite village.

Further information

St Thomas à Becket church was founded in 1180. There are several grave covers in the porch which indicate that a church existed in early Norman times. The church contains the tomb of Amy Woodforde Finden, composer of 'Kashmiri Song' from Four Indian Love Lyrics. The porch was erected to the memory of William Makepeace Thackeray.

Ripley Castle has been the residence of the Ingilby family for 650 years. It is open to the public from May to September on Sundays and Bank holidays.

Hampsthwaite is an ancient settlement of the Brigantes; it was the site of an important river crossing in Roman times.

Hardraw Force

START The National Park Centre car park, Hawes, DL8 3NT, GR SD875900

DISTANCE Short route 4 miles (6.5km); long route 7 miles (11km)

SUMMARY Moderate/hard; some rougher walking on the longer circuit

MAPS OS Explorer OL30 Yorkshire Dales: Northern and Central Areas; OS Landranger 98 Wensleydale & Upper Wharfedale

WHERE TO EAT AND DRINK
The Green Dragon, Hardraw, T01969-667392; lots of hotels, pubs and cafés in Hawes, including Herriots (T01969-667536)

A splendid walk along field and fell paths with some steep climbs, and the highest waterfall in England.

[1] From the National Park Centre cross the disused railway line and take the path to Brunt Acres Rd. Turn right for 75yds. Now follow a path on your left marked 'Pennine Way', crossing two fields diagonally on paved stones to rejoin the road. Continue north along the road, crossing the River Ure and, about ¼ mile further on where the road climbs, turn left over a stile at a 'Pennine Way' signpost.

[2] Take the paved path westward, over stiles and through pastures, reaching Hardraw village opposite the Green Dragon Inn. Detour here through the inn, for a small charge, and go up either side of Fossdale Beck to spectacular Hardraw Force. Back at the inn go left through the back yard of the end cottage and climb the steep, flagged path up a field. Here, the views of Upper Wensleydale are excellent and embrace Yorburgh (1,686ft/514m) and Wether Fell (2,015ft/614m). When you reach the top of the field cross a stile, then climb again along a fenced path to West House, where you turn right through a gated stile.

[3] The shorter alternative route of 4 miles takes the path from here to the hilltop hamlet of Simonstone and continues through a series of stiled fields to Sedbusk, rejoining the main route there.

[4] From West House the main route goes up the farm track to the Buttertubs Rd and left along it to a signpost indicating 'Shaw Sill

Wood'. Go down the enclosed path and cross a footbridge to explore enchanting Sylvan Shaw Gill and its waterfalls. Upstream, cross another footbridge and turn left, then right, through a wall. Go right down a lane to a hamlet of High Shaw and back to the Buttertubs Rd. Turn left along this unfenced moorland road for 2 miles of marvellous uphill walking, framed by stunning views.

5 When, just past Shivery Gill on the right, a bridleway signposted 'Sedbusk 2½ miles' is reached, turn right and climb steeply onto Abbotside Common. The way, at first, is undefined: go right over deep, rocky Shivery Gill and continue in a south-easterly direction along Pike Hill which, at 1,700ft above sea level, will thrill you with panoramic views that enfold the fells of Great Shunner, Wether, Dodd and Widdale, with distant Ingleborough and Whernside thrown in for good measure. Continue along the escarpment, keeping well to the left of four clearly seen cairns. As you pass them, wheel eastwards, keeping well back from steep Hill Clint. At the eastern end of the escarpment descend to join a track which will take you through a gate, half-left across a pasture. Go through another gate and down a sunken track to a walled enclosure with trees. Turn right by the trees, go down a rutted track and over a stile into Shutt La. Go right along the walled lane for ¼ mile into the hamlet of Sedbusk.

6 The shorter route rejoins here. At the foot of the hamlet go right along the road. Cross the stile on your left signposted 'Haylands Bridge' and cross stiled fields to the Hardraw–Askrigg Rd. Cross and go over a stile to follow another signposted path over more stiled fields. Go over a hump-back bridge, then cross another field to reach Brunt Acres Rd.
Turn left along it
back into Hawes.

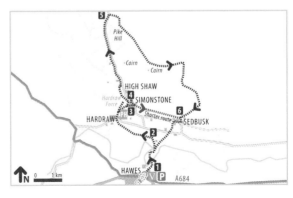

Scar House Reservoir

START Scar House Reservoir car park, HG3 5SW (nearby), GR SE069766

DISTANCE 4 miles (6.5km)

SUMMARY Easy walking, but strong footwear recommended

MAPS OS Explorer 298 Nidderdale; OS Landranger 98 Wensleydale & Upper Wharfedale, and 99 Northallerton & Ripon

WHERE TO EAT AND DRINK
The Crown Hotel (T01423-755206) at Lofthouse is the nearest place for a snack; Pateley Bridge is 8 miles down the valley

A beautiful, short walk with great views over the two reservoirs that populate the Upper Nidderdale valley.

[1]   From the car park walk past the stone cottages, now used as storage places, to the dam. Note the modern memorial to the navvies here. The plaque to commemorate the official opening of the reservoir is at the beginning of the dam. Walk across to the opposite shore. You may see swifts round the towers and oyster catchers closer to the water.

[2]   Turn left on the rough track and follow it alongside the reservoir. A steep track goes diagonally up to the right to a viewpoint at the old quarry – a rewarding diversion for the more adventurous. At a copse of trees are the ruins of the hamlet of Stone. Just beyond the trees there is a T-junction where a packhorse track comes down from Coverdale. Turn left, go through the gate and follow the path across the field to reach the top dam.

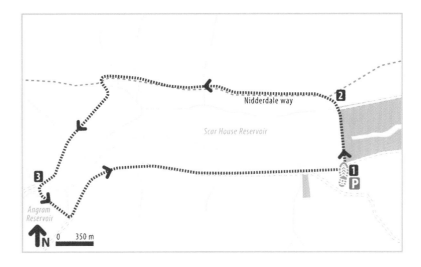

[3] Go across the dam. To the right is the smaller Y-shaped reservoir of Angram where there is a colony of Canada geese. Beyond rises the peak of Great Whernside. At the far side of the dam go past a stone shelter with gates to keep the sheep out. Turn left and return by the waterworks road by Scar Reservoir to the car park. In the frequent damp patches bog cotton flowers. Lapwings and curlews are often heard, and in warm weather there can be adders about. Just before the car park, a track is seen winding over the hill to the right. This is a continuation of the packhorse track, which goes to Middlesmoor.

Points of interest

The village of Middlesmoor is prominent on the hilltop above Lofthouse; from its churchyard is one of the finest views in Nidderdale. Scar House Reservoir supplies the Bradford area as one of three reservoirs in Upper Nidderdale.

WALK

10 Raydale

START The Carlow Stone, DL8 3DJ,
GR SD922876 (parking at the Semer
Water car park, north-east of the lake)

DISTANCE 4 miles (6.5km)

SUMMARY Easy walking, mainly
along field paths and lanes

MAPS OS Explorer OL30
Yorkshire Dales: Northern and
Central Areas; OS Landranger 98
Wensleydale & Upper Wharfedale

WHERE TO EAT AND DRINK
Bainbridge is 2 miles from Semer
Water; the Corn Mill Tea Room (T01969-
650212) has excellent sandwiches; The
Rose & Crown Hotel (T01969-650735)

A short walk around Semer Water, with views into upper Raydale.

[1] If you stand at the Carlow Stone facing the lake, the way is left
for ½ mile along the road as far as Low Blean Farm, where you turn
right over a ladder stile opposite, signposted 'Stalling Busk 1 mile'.
Go south-westerly from the stile, following yellow markers across
pastures, over three stiles, cradled in beautiful countryside, and with
Addlebrough (1,564ft/477m) at your back. The way is past a barn on
your left, close to the lake on your right. As Semer Water slips behind,
you climb gradually across rough pasture on a good, signposted path
going through three gated stiles to ruinous Stalling Busk Church. On
leaving the church, turn right and straight away go half-left through
a gap in a broken wall where a signpost marked 'Stalling Busk' points
the way uphill. After ½ mile the hamlet of Stalling Busk is reached,
perched at the top of a 200ft climb.

[2] Once in the hamlet, turn right, then bear left to have a look at the
Church of St Matthew. From the church bear right to unsignposted
Busk La opposite and continue along it, descending steeply to cross
Cragdale Beck on a concrete bridge. Turn right, keeping close to
the beck, and make your way across muddy, low-lying ground to
a footbridge over Raydale Beck. Continue straight ahead, crossing
Longdale Sike on a slab bridge, and aim for a stile beside a gate.

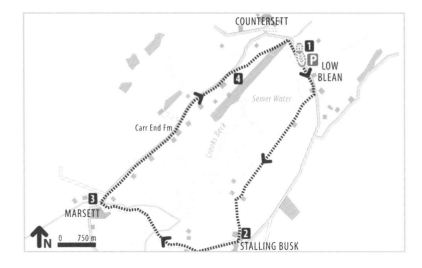

Go over and along the lane ahead, with Marsett Beck on your right, to the green in Marsett hamlet.

③   Turn right, crossing Marsett Bridge and keep on Marsett La, which you have just joined, for a good mile, passing Carr End Farm after ½ mile on your right. The views over Semer Water are enchanting and you can pick out the part you have already walked and admire Stalling Busk from a distance.

④   About ½ mile past Carr End Farm, where the lane descends, cross the signposted stile on your right and take a route identified by yellow markers for ¼ mile across a field and by a woodside beck to a gate close to Semer Water Bridge on your right. Turn right here and follow the road skirting the lake back to the Carlow Stone.

Points of interest

The Carlow Stone and the nearby Mermaid Stones are said to have been thrown at each other by the devil and a giant from hills on opposite sides of the lake. Couples thinking about getting married are drawn to the Carlow Stone, because tradition has it that touching it will bring prosperity and many children.

11 Upper Wharfedale

START Townfoot Bridge car park, Kettlewell, BD23 5QX, GR SD967723

DISTANCE 4 miles (6.5km)

SUMMARY A short walk with some stiles to cross that follows the Wharf in Upper Wharfedale

MAPS OS Explorer OL30 Yorkshire Dales: Northern and Central Areas; OS Landranger 98 Wensleydale & Upper Wharfedale

WHERE TO EAT AND DRINK The Bluebell (T01756-760230) and the Racehorses (T01756-760233) are two typical friendly Dales pubs on the bridge in Kettlewell – walkers, dogs and children all welcome

A short walk with some stiles to cross that follows the river in Upper Wharfedale.

[1] Cross the small bridge into the village and follow the road up the left side of the Bluebell Hotel. Where the road turns right, go straight ahead, over a stile, then turn left along the wall-side. This path follows the route of a Roman road from Ilkley, up Wharfedale over Stake Pass to Bainbridge and on to Catterick. Drystone walls enclose the small fields and there are stiles to be negotiated. The path is more or less level along the lower edge of an old wood, Cross Wood. The track sloping diagonally up the opposite side of the dale led to the Moor End lead mines.

[2] At the third barn (Calfhalls) past the wood, angle left down to Starbotton village. Pause to look round the village and note the mullioned cottage with its date stone of 1656. Cross the road, B6160, to a short path to the footbridge, with flood markers.

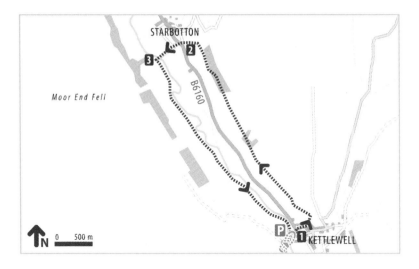

③ Cross the bridge and follow the well-signposted Dales Way
to the left, downstream to Kettlewell. Riverside birds include grey
wagtails and sandpipers. Down the dale the overhang of Kilnsey Crag,
popular with rock climbers, can be seen. There are numerous rabbits
in this area, including black ones. Take time to explore Kettlewell.
A stroll through its quiet lanes and turnings reveals a number of
seventeenth- and eighteenth-century cottages. Lovely gardens run
down to the beck. The church is late Victorian. There are three inns
and various tearooms.

Points of interest

The Scarecrow Festival in Kettlewell, held in mid-August, is a great day
out for the family. Seemingly all the village makes a great effort and
there is a trail to follow.

Ingleton Waterfalls

START Public car park at
the foot of the Triss Valley,
BD23 1NJ, GR SD693733

DISTANCE 4½ miles (7km)

SUMMARY A rough but enjoyable
walk next to the rivers Doe and Triss

MAPS OS Explorer OL2 Yorkshire
Dales: Southern and Western
Areas; OS Landranger 98
Wensleydale & Upper Wharfedale

INFORMATION Trail access costs £14
for a family and £6 for a single adult.
The walk is very well signposted, but
they sometimes redirect walkers so it
is best to closely follow the sign posts

WHERE TO EAT AND DRINK There
is a refreshment stall high up in
the Triss Valley but it's only open in
summer and at weekends; otherwise
there is a large choice in Ingleton

A wonderful set of waterfalls rise to the limestone plateau of Whernside and offer
an interesting few hours of walking.

1   Leave the car park and head through the woods (oak and ash) of
Swilla Glen. After ½ mile cross the River Twiss and exit near the first
of the waterfalls, Pecca Force. This is typical limestone scenery, with
heathers and brackens overlooking the five waterfalls. For another
¾ mile the path climbs steeply through the woods before entering
more open moorland. At this stage there is a refreshment hut.

2   The path follows the river for another 200yds, past Thornton
Falls, before meeting an obvious road. This is an old Roman road
(Twisleton La) and for ½ mile it follows a direct line, passing Scar End
Farm and Twisleton Hall before crossing a road.

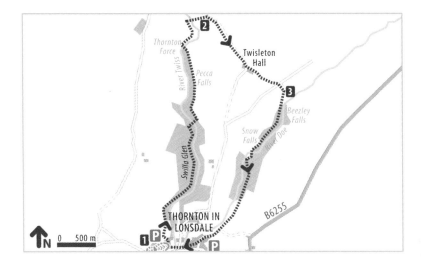

③ A gate and path leads down to the River Doe. The Doe drops over a series of spectacular waterfalls, including the Beezley and Rival Falls. Sometimes the young and keen can be seen jumping and diving in to the deep pools, offering a spectacular backdrop to the natural beauty. The path crosses to the east bank above Snow Falls and then the route starts to flatten out. The final ¾ mile is through open limestone country till the path meets the houses on the outskirts of the village. After 200yds you will arrive at the main street of Ingleton; turn right and cross the bridge back to the car park.

Points of interest

Ingleton boasts a Hoffman kiln, cotton mills, an eighteenth-century agricultural barn and other features, giving the place a real historical feel.

Knox Hall & Smelthouses

START The lane adjacent to Knox
Hall (not in the restaurant's private
car park), outskirts of Smelthouses,
HG3 4DQ, GR SE191640

DISTANCE 4½ miles (7km)

SUMMARY Easy

MAPS OS Explorer 298
Nidderdale; OS Landranger
99 Northallerton & Ripon

WHERE TO EAT AND DRINK
The Royal Oak Inn, Dacre village,
T01423-780200, walkers and children
welcome; The Darley Mill, B6451
to Harrogate Rd (T01423-780857)

A nice easy walk with superb views and historical interest.

[1]   Follow the lane at the eastern side of Knox Hall through the wood
to Smelthouses. Turn left over the bridge and almost immediately join
the track on your right, signposted 'Whitehouses', that winds through
the wood before descending to the side of Fell Beck. Walk upstream
and cross over the wooden bridge above a small dam. Bear right,
uphill, for 80yds but then do not go past the building on your right.
Instead, turn sharp left onto a narrow path leading to a stile in the
stone wall. Keeping to the general line of the beck, but on top of the
escarpment, reach the walled green lane near Low Wood Farm.

[2]   Cross over the lane to the stile opposite and go through the small
copse to an opening in the next wall, partially hidden by a large holly
tree. On entering the field bordered by an indistinct sunken green
track, bear left downhill and cross Fell Beck over a wooden bridge
below the dam. Go over a wooden stile and proceed uphill for 70yds
along the farm track before turning left over the cattle grid into a field.
Go forward along the track to Grove Cottage.

[3]   Go over the stile at the left of the cottage and turn left along the
lane towards Whitehouses. When you reach a junction with another
lane coming from the right, cross straight over to the gate opposite,
which gives access to a green track meandering westwards roughly
parallel to the main road above.

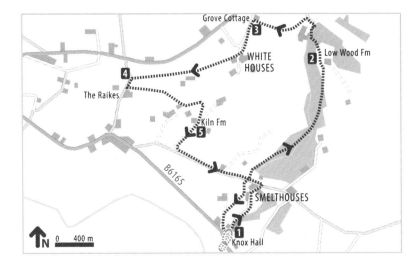

④ Continue along the track, which exits onto a steep metalled road. At a sharp bend turn left down the road to Raikes and join the narrow path between two properties on the left that will take you to Kiln. Keep to the north-east side of the buildings at Kiln, bear left up the farm road and then sharp right at the junction.

⑤ Pass Kiln Farm and continue down the road. Turn left along the road towards Smelthouses, but instead of crossing the bridge to rejoin the lane to Knox Manor, take the footpath on the right alongside one of the houses into the field above the beck. Follow the beck downstream and join the farm drive from Old Wall House back to Knox Hall.

Points of interest

The cottages at Smelthouses are a picture in springtime and summer. This was the location of the earliest flax mill in Nidderdale, established in 1798. As its name suggests, there was a lead smelting mill here in the middle of the fourteenth century.

Walking towards Grove Cottage, turn round – you will see all the mystical shapes of the famous Brimham Rocks.

Malham Tarn

START Street Gate,
BD24 9PU, GR SD904656

DISTANCE 4½ miles (7km)

SUMMARY Medium difficulty
walk unless you decide to
tackle Gordale Scar, in which
case it would be difficult

MAPS OS Explorer OL2 Yorkshire
Dales: Southern and Western
Areas; OS Landranger 98
Wensleydale & Upper Wharfedale

WHERE TO EAT AND DRINK
Malham has two country inns: the
Buck Inn (T01729-830317) and the
Listers Arms (T01729-830330)

A walk round the country's highest lake along quiet Herriot roads, a nature
reserve and limestone scenery.

[1] Park on the side of the road at Street Gate (there is plenty of
space) and then head due north on the Landrover track signed to
Middle House. After ¾ mile a copse on the left signifies a left-hand
fork towards the tarn. The path is soon obvious as it skirts some
spectacular limestone scars to your right. When the tarn is reached,
there is a few hundred yards of splendid lakeside walking before a gate
signifies a change of scenery and woodland.

[2] Bear left through the gate and follow the path for a few hundred
yards to the National Trust field centre. Pass between the buildings
and re-enter the woods. There are intermittent views of the lake from
some specially placed bird hides. As the path drops to the waterside, a
house appears (the start of a few, collectively known as Water Houses)
and a nature reserve is signposted.

[3] Take this (unless you have a dog, in which case carry on and take
the minor road beside High Trenhouse) and with a mixture of paths
and boards cross through the reserve. There are a number of signs
explaining what you may or may not see.

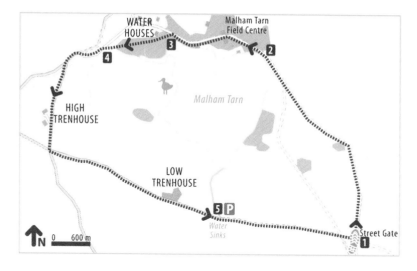

④ Where the reserve meets a minor road, turn left until there is a junction. Take the left fork and pass High Trenhouse (an outdoor centre) before another junction in ½ mile. At this point turn left and you are on the road that leads back to Street Gate, 1½ miles away. This is a lovely road, without any boundaries on either side; for much of the way it is classic Yorkshire Dales.

⑤ After 1 mile there is a cattle grid and stream entering from the tarn. It is worth following the stream south for an extra ¾-mile round-trip to Water Sinks (see box) before returning the same way to the road. Carry on as the road rises slightly and you will soon arrive back at Street Gate.

Points of interest

Water Sinks: created by the limestone bedrock, the stream from Malham Tarn disappears in a hole for hundreds of feet before appearing near the foot of Malham Cove a mile downstream.

The National Trust Visitor Centre is a popular destination for schools and other outdoor groups and has a fine nature reserve.

Linton & Hebden Riverside

START Outside the Fountaine Inn at Linton, BD23 5HJ, GR SD 998628

DISTANCE 4½ miles (7km)

SUMMARY Easy/moderate.

MAPS OS Explorer OL2; Landranger 98.

WHERE TO EAT AND DRINK
The Fountaine Inn at Linton (T01756-752210); the Old School Tea Room at Hebden (T01756-753778) breaks the walk at half point.

This walk takes in the three pretty villages of Linton, Hebden and Thorpe, with some attractive riverside walking between

1 Park in the centre of the small village within site of the Fountaine Inn. Cross the river to the east bank and turn right and head along the lane for 100yds. Turn left up another lane and follow the wall (on your left-hand side) as it climbs steadily up some sheep-grazing fields. Pass between two copses before crossing three stiles. Keep heading south-east till arriving at a walled lane. Enter Thorpe La and turn left. Follow this for ½ mile before entering the small village of Thorpe (the pub here is closed, but look for the sign on one of the house walls on your left).

2 Where the lane meets a road in Thorpe, turn right and then soon left to follow the quiet road as it heads towards the River Wharfe. At a further road junction, cross directly opposite and take the bridleway directly down the hill. The path soon arrives at a spectacular suspension bridge which crosses the river. Over the bridge the path you want turns left and follows the river but it is worth carrying on up the hill, joining a road which leads in to the village of Hebden. Hebden is an old and attractive mining village, many buildings now converted to holiday cottages. Return the way you came to the suspension bridge.

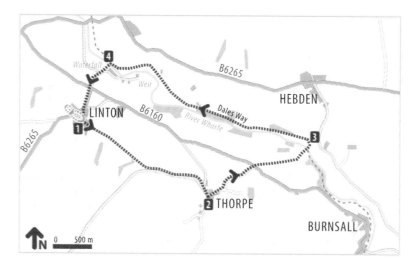

3. The path, heading west towards Grassington, sticks close to the river for 1 mile until it passes some sewage works to the left. Head inland past some wonderfully situated houses by the river, before dropping back to the river front via a path to your left. After ½ mile you arrive at the bridge at Linton Falls.

4. The footbridge at Linton Falls is a spectacular place. The waters of the Wharfe cascade mightily under the bridge, used in the past to power one of the old industrial mills. Once over the bridge, turn sharp right then left to climb away from the old mill (now converted) buildings. Climb up a quiet road as you head back towards Linton. At a road junction cross and continue to head up the hill, arriving back at your start point in the village of Linton.

Points of interest

The River Wharfe forms a major part of the Dales Way which heads up valley to its source miles away above the village of Hawes. Travelling downstream the river joins the River Ouse before heading east to the sea.

16 Dacre Banks

START School Lane (near the
youth hostel), Dacre Banks,
HG3 4EN, GR SE195616

DISTANCE 5 miles (8km)

SUMMARY Easy

MAPS OS Explorer 298
Nidderdale; OS Landranger
99 Northallerton & Ripon

WHERE TO EAT AND DRINK
The Royal Oak Inn, Dacre village
(T01423-780200), walkers and children
welcome; The Darley Mill, B6451
to Harrogate Rd (T01423-780857)

A varied walk over fields and moor and through woodland, with an easy climb and great views over Lower Nidderdale.

1 Pass the youth hostel at the end of School La and cross the cattle grid onto the farm road. Turn left uphill at the junction just past the bridge and walk through the farmyard to join a green track that begins at the left-hand side of a large slurry tank. Follow this track uphill as it bends to the right and turn left through the second gateway. Continue with the wall on your left to the wooden stile in the perimeter fence of the second field. Climb over the stile in the stone wall ahead. Bear right across the middle of this next field, walking uphill towards the gate at the top, leading onto a rough lane. Continue up to the crossroads.

2 Turn right toward Heyshaw, passing the entrance to Lane Foot Farm on the left. At the bottom of the lane go through the wooden gate and pass between the two buildings to reach a metal gate. Go through into a field and continue beside a fence on your left, where you will soon discover signs of an old paved way. These stone slabs lead to a narrow gate. Pass through the adjoining wide gateway and follow the paved path towards the farm at the top of the field.

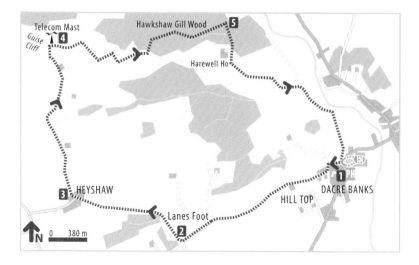

③ Bear to the right of the silage bay to a stile onto the lane at Heyshaw. Walk up the lane, turn right along the rough track towards Guise Cliff and go through the wooden gate onto Heyshaw Moor. Follow the moorland road to the Telecom mast on the skyline. Bear left round the mast, go over the stile near the wall and, following the wall on the right, go through the small gap on to Guise Cliff. From this point there are splendid views back along the dale to Great Whernside and eastward to Brimham Rocks and the Hambleton Hills beyond. In the woods below is tiny Guise Cliff Tarn and many more delightful paths to explore for those who have time to spare.

④ From the top of Guise Cliff follow the right-hand track down to wire fencing. Turn right along the track to a stile. Go straight ahead to another stile, turn left down the field, walk along the bottom to a stile in the wall on the left by a gate, and follow the wall down to a stile in the corner. Follow the track through Hawkshaw Gill Wood.

⑤ At the T-junction turn right and at the fork junction turn right again. Go up to and through a gate, along a field and through another gate to a gate next to the farmhouse of Harewell House Farm. Keep left through the farm and go down the farm lane. Keep right at the junction by the stream to return to School La.

17 Gunnerside Gill

START Gunnerside, DL11 6LE,
GR SD952983 (park next to the
river; if full, you may have to
park outside the village)

DISTANCE 5 miles (8km)

SUMMARY Easy walking alongside
the river on a good path

MAPS OS Explorer OL30
Yorkshire Dales: Northern and
Central Areas; OS Landranger 92
Barnard Castle & Richmond & 98
Wensleydale & Upper Wharfedale

WHERE TO EAT AND DRINK The
Kings Head (T01748-886261), the tea
shop (T01748-886409) and Farmers
Arms (T01748-886297) at Muker. The
Punch Bowl in Low Row has high
quality dining (T01969-650113)

A walk up and returning beside Gunnerside Gill by the beck side, to the
Sir Francis lead mines.

1   Going over the bridge, turn left along a track by the beck,
opposite the Kings Head Inn. Follow the track to a Gunnerside Gill
sign, turning right up eight steps. Pass through a handgate, bear left to
follow the beckside to another handgate to woodland, and go through
keeping to the path along the beckside. The large boulders around this
area were deposited by free flooding over the centuries. Walk about
300yds to a gated stile on the right and climb the steps. Continue
ahead, passing a 'Woodland Path' sign into the wood. Follow this path,
going over a wooden stile, to where two stone stiles lead into a field.
With the wall on your left, go over two more stiles.

2   After a short distance you reach the remains of the Sir Francis
mining complex, a worthwhile break point to look and ponder. This
site is quiet now, but in the 1800s it was full of activity. Continuing our
walk, we follow the waymarks alongside the stream. Cross over the
stile, go up to a track from the mine on the side of the gill, climb over
a wooden stile and walk until you reach a stone stile. At this point,
looking across the beck, the ruined buildings you see are those of the

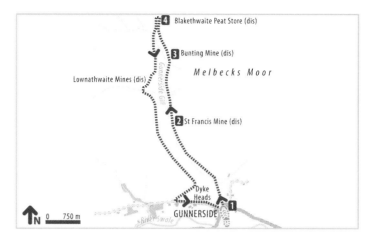

mine office and stables. Go over the stile and follow a well-defined track for about ¾ mile.

3   The ruins you now come to are the Bunting mines, which were formerly the offices, stables, blacksmith's, gunpowder stores and the water wheel pit. Across the valley you can see the Dolly mine. From this point you follow the beckside for a further ¾ mile or so to reach the remains of Blakethwaite peat store and smelt mill.

4   Cross the stone slab bridge over the beck and follow the well-defined bridle path that takes you along the side of the valley back towards Gunnerside, passing Lownathwaite mines and Dolly lead level. Follow the path to Dyke Heads, turning left at the track road to reach Gunnerside.

Points of interest

The name Gunnerside is Norse and means the shieling (derelict hut usually used by shepherds) of Gunner. Lead mining flourished in the eighteenth and nineteenth centuries; in 1851, 180 villagers were employed in the mines. The Bunting and Lownathwaite mines comprise one of the richest ore-bearing complexes in Swaledale. The fields in this area are some of the oldest enclosures in Swaledale. Many of the barns seen on the walk are relics of the eighteenth and early nineteenth centuries, an era in which many miners had smallholdings on which they kept a few sheep or a cow or two.

Masham, Leighton & Druid's Temple

START Market Square, Masham (voluntary payment), HG4 4DY, GR SE806227

DISTANCE Short route 5 miles (8km); long route 11 miles (18km)

SUMMARY Moderate; pleasant walking on good paths or lanes

MAPS OS Explorer OL302 Northallerton & Thirsk; OS Landranger 99 Northallerton & Ripon

WHERE TO EAT AND DRINK There is a very large choice in the centre of Masham, including Fancy That Tea Room (T01765-688161) and the White Bear (T01765-689319)

A walk along the River Burn towards the folly at Druids Temple and returning via Leighton. A shorter version is also available.

① From Masham Market Square go along Silver St, and opposite Brownless Garage take the signposted path to a sports ground where you turn right. Continue by the river, then through a waymarked wood, exiting over a stile. Pass a house and turn left onto a surfaced lane. Go along it, passing a lane on the left, and continue along an unsurfaced lane to join a riverside path for ½ mile to the meeting of the Ure and Burn Rivers.

② Turn right, crossing a stile into a wood and following the path by the River Burn to Low Burn Bridge. Cross the bridge and then a stile on your right to join a riverside path and continue along it to Masham Golf Course, reached over a stile. Continue along the edge of the golf course to Swinton Bridge. Cross and go through a wicket gate on your left. Pass in front of the clubhouse and continue along a riverside path to the end of the golf course. Exit over a stile, climb the side of a fenced field and go along a gated farm road towards Shaw's Farm, turning right by the outbuildings. Follow waymarkers past the farm, going through a gate and bearing half right, aiming for the middle of some transmission poles seen ahead. Ignoring the gate on your right, go through the one ahead and take the path to Micklebury La. For shorter route turn right here.

③ Turn left down the lane and right along Low Moor La for

1½ miles. Turn left at the lane end, cross the River Burn and continue along the road for an uphill road walk of ½ mile to where, at the 'No Through Road' symbol, you go right into Knowle La and follow a 'Druid's Wood' sign westward for 1 mile to Druid's Plantation. Take the path signposted 'Viewpoint' to a hilltop folly resembling a miniature Stonehenge called the Druid's Temple.

4   Return down Knowle La for a few hundred yards and go left first through two gates. Turn left along the edge of the wood and left again through a further gate between plantations. Now go right, with Knowle Plantation on your right, to join a track going through a gate into a field. Cross this along a track to join a path from Broadmines. Go left along the path to cross Potts Beck on a packhorse bridge and climb steeply out of the valley and through a facing gate. Turn right up the field to an old barn and go right through a gate. Cross the field to exit through a gate into Leighton hamlet.

5   Turn right along the road for 1½ miles to Healey and, beyond the school, turn right and continue to the junction on your left. Turn into Low Moor La, which you walked on the outward route. When, after 1½ miles, it bifurcates, turn left along Micklebury La, passing the spot where the outward route joined it.

6   Opposite where a lane branches diagonally on the left, go through a gate on the right and follow yellow waymarkers for the final 1½ miles back to Masham (see Walk 1), passing Theakston's Brewery (hardest part of the walk!) and turning left along Red La into the Market Square.

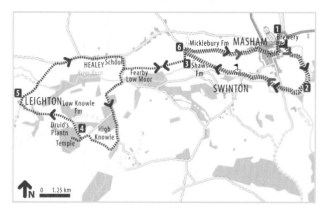

Numberstones End from Burnsall

START Burnsall, BD23 6BU,
GR SE033613

DISTANCE 5 miles (8km)

SUMMARY Moderate; a steep climb
makes this a bit of a challenge

MAPS OS Explorer OL2
Yorkshire Dales: Southern and
Western Areas; OS Landranger
103 Blackburn & Burnley

WHERE TO EAT AND DRINK
The Red Lion Inn (T01756-720204)
and the Wharfe View Tea Rooms
(T01756-720237) are good choices

A steep climb for a superb view of Wharfedale, with an easy return through level
pastures.

1 Numberstones End is the steep crag to the south of the village,
up which a fell race is held each summer. The route described here is a
much easier one, starting along the Bolton Abbey road, but leaving it
500yds further on where the plantation begins.

2 The steep track on the right through the woods provides access
to Barden Moor (unless shooting is in progress). The track takes you
to the south corner of the wood, where you cross a stile to reach the
moor. Turn back right, along the wall, until, on arriving at the far
corner of the wood, you can look down on Burnsall. Turn back now,
to the south, climbing steeply on a good green track. On reaching a
little plateau, turn right through the bracken to reach a rocky gully,
from which you emerge to find an extensive view over Wharfedale.
The track continues as a hollow way, curving round the northern
shoulder of the hill.

3 When the way becomes indistinct, continue forward to join a fell-
runners' track from Burnsall. Turn left and follow it to a ridge leading
to the prominent cairn ahead. This splendid viewpoint is not the
summit, so continue along a narrow but distinct track which hugs the
top of the steep slopes falling to your right. Arriving at another cairn
– the real summit of Numberstones End – make for the shooting box
ahead (due west), either by taking a straight line through the heather,

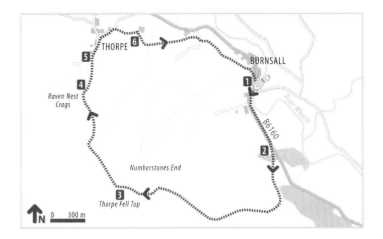

or by turning south-west to join a wide sandy track which takes you to the same place.

4 At the shooting box, leave the main track by turning right along a smaller one at right-angles, which passes a filled-in coal pit and then starts to descend, becoming a deep hollow way as it does so. Follow it, with many changes in direction to avoid the most difficult ground, past a cairn and a disused stone quarry, to the moor wall, from which point the name Thorpe-in-the-Hollow, sometimes given to the village below, is seen to be most appropriate.

5 Go through the gate into the walled lane, and follow it down into the village. Fork right at the bottom and follow the lane up to the brow of the hill. There, fork right again, along the walled green lane signposted to Burnsall.

6 Where the lane ends, turn right over the stile then go down to the gate below. On passing through it, veer left to reach the stile in the bottom corner of the field. Cross the plank bridge and go up the field beyond, keeping the barn well to your right. Pass through two gap stiles in succession to reach Badger La, which you cross at right-angles and go straight on. Burnsall now appears in view ahead, and is reached by crossing a number of well-built stone stiles. On emerging, through a yard, into the main street, turn right to return to Burnsall bridge and green.

Reeth Low Moor

START Reeth, DL11 6SW, GR NZ038993

DISTANCE 5 miles (8km)

SUMMARY Moderate

MAPS OS Explorer OL30
Yorkshire Dales: Northern and
Central Areas; OS Landranger 92
Barnard Castle & Richmond & 98
Wensleydale & Upper Wharfedale

WHERE TO EAT AND DRINK
There are a number of pubs and
cafés in Reeth; try the Buck Inn
(T01748-884210), which has hand-
pulled ales and excellent food

A walk onto the moor above Reeth, with a combination of tracks, some riverside
paths and a short climb.

[1]   Leave Reeth by the Gunnerside road. As the buildings of Reeth are
left behind, a narrow enclosed lane signposted 'Skellgate' will be visible
on the right. Turn up this lane, which runs between stone walls over the
Riddings Farm road, to reach open moor via a wooden gate. The track
accompanies a stone wall on the left and heads off across the moor.

[2]   When the stone wall turns down to Riddings Farm, continue
straight on over the moor until eventually the wall comes back to
rejoin the track. Shortly after the wall is rejoined, look for a green
track heading up the moor on the right. Follow this as it climbs
gradually up to Calver Hill: a broken down stone wall points the way
to the summit of the hill. Leave the summit heading westward and,
when a crumbling wall appears on your left, head towards it. Pass the
wall, heading directly down the moor, keeping a corrugated tin hut on
your left. On reaching a clear path cross straight over to another clear
path and turn left to follow it down to the pretty village of Healaugh.
Walk straight through the village to reach the main road running
along Swaledale. Turn left.

[3]   As you reach the end of the village a green appears on the right.
Here, a signposted path to Reeth and Grinton runs from the barn
corner. Follow the path through a metal gate into a meadow and

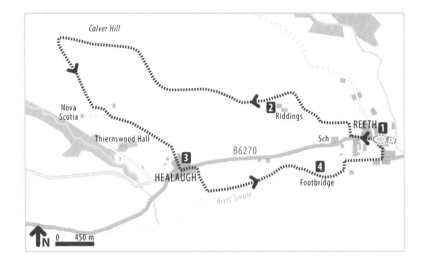

alongside the left-hand wall to the river. Turn left at the river and follow the path to a suspension bridge.

④ Do not cross the bridge, but go through a gate in the stone wall and follow the path as it heads away from the river. Cross a wooden footbridge turning right and, almost immediately, turn left at a signpost and pass through a wooden gate into an enclosed lane. Follow the lane as it moves towards the outskirts of Reeth. After a right-angled turn right, ignore the first public footpath sign on your left and continue along the lane until it starts to descend. A lane on your left, with a sign for Hilary House on the corner, is where you leave the lane. Turn left at this point and follow the lane into Reeth.

Points of interest

Healaugh village telephone box is quite an attraction, with a carpet, directories and fresh flowers – do leave a donation.

Reeth market, granted by charter in the sixth year of William and Mary's reign, is on Fridays, and fairs are held on the Friday before Good Friday, on Old May-day, Old Midsummer-day, the festival of St Bartholomew, Old Martinmas-day, and St Thomas' day.

Richmond & Hudswell

START Richmond Market Place, DL10 4HS, GR NZ169010

DISTANCE 5 miles (8 km)

SUMMARY Easy

MAPS OS Explorer 304 Darlington & Richmond; OS Landranger 92 Barnard Castle & Richmond

WHERE TO EAT AND DRINK There is a vast choice in Richmond but pop into the dog-friendly George and Dragon (T01748-518373) at Hudswell during the walk

A riverside stroll along the River Swale, visiting the pretty village of Hudsworth. The walk spends considerable time in attractive woodland.

1 From Richmond Market Place go along New Rd for a few yards into The Bar, a narrow lane. Continue down cobbled Cornforth Hill and Bridge St to cross the River Swale on Green Bridge. Turn right between the bridge and a corner cottage into Billy Bank Wood.

2 Take the broad riverside path upstream, ignoring a right track after 150yds. Keep to the main path, climb some steps and continue up a stony, woodland path. Branch right along a level path leading to a plank bridge, crossing a beck close to a 'Hudswell Woods' sign. Keeping to the main path, descend through lovely woodland to cross a stile near a National Trust sign and turn left along a riverside meadow. The partly hidden cave you pass on your left is called Arthur's Oven. Beyond the meadow, cross a waymarked stile and go half-right to join a riverside path, from where a wooded conical hill, Round Howe, is seen.

3 Pass the metal footbridge spanning the Swale on your right and continue for 1 mile along the river bank into Calfhall Wood, to where your path goes half-left, away from the river, to leave the wood at a Public Footpath sign near a pumping station. Turn left and climb 328 Steps, at the top of which there is a choice of routes.

4 Either turn left along the top of Calfhall Wood or climb a few more steps, cross a stile and go up the path into Hudswell, a hilltop

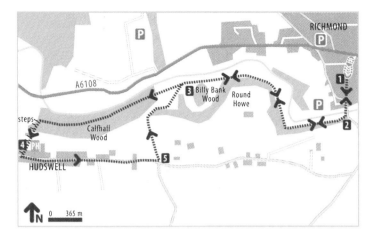

village with a friendly pub, The George and Dragon. Turn left through the village where, just beyond the old school, there is a footpath sign fixed to a wall between Random House and Norley.

5 Turn left here, down a lane, to cross a field, then a stile near a gate. Bear left alongside a fence to join the path that has come directly from the step's top, turning right along it to cross a watercourse. Go over a stile. Where the path ends, climb wooden steps, cross a stile and go left along the edge of a field to another stile leading back into the wood. Continue along the top of the wood, ignoring the stile on your right, and leave it using a stile. Continue along a rutted track, downhill, past a 'Public Footpath' fixed to an ancient oak, to return to the metal footbridge over the Swale. Go right, briefly, and turn left over a waymarked stile near a gate and continue along the riverside. At the far end of the meadow cross a stile onto an enclosed path under Billy Bank Wood, using limestone slabs to rejoin the outward route of this excellent walk. Retrace your steps out of the wood and back to the start of the walk in Richmond Market Place.

Points of interest

The 328 Steps were made by German prisoners during World War II to link the pumping station to the treatment plant above.

WALKS

23
24

Richmond Circular

START Car park on the Green, below
Culloden Tower, Richmond Bridge,
Richmond, DL10 4QW, GR NZ168007

DISTANCE Short route 5 miles
(8km); long route 7 miles (11km)

SUMMARY An easy walk with
the Swale river, waterfalls
and ancient monuments

MAPS OS Explorer 304 Darlington
& Richmond; OS Landranger 92
Barnard Castle & Richmond

WHERE TO EAT AND DRINK
A large choice of pubs, hotels
and cafés in Richmond

Both of these walks offer a wonderful choice array of ancient sites and modern scenery. Richmond is a bustling market town set on the fringes of the Dales.

[1] Leave the car park and follow the road across the Green to Richmond Bridge. Turn left before crossing the bridge and follow the road skirting the river to the impressive waterfalls below the castle. Please note, the Swale is one of the fastest flowing rivers in Britain and can flood rapidly; take notice of all warning signs. Continue following the riverside footpaths until you reach Station Bridge. Pass under this and follow the path almost on the water's edge for 100yds until you have to turn left. Follow a short lane until it turns right with a footpath sign pointing to Easby Abbey. It's about ¾ mile to the remains of this Premonstratensian (a branch of the Cistercian order) House, which is open to the public.

[2] After a couple of hundred yards the path splits. Take the left-hand one and follow it to the Abbey: your return route can be on the other path, which is closer to the river bank. Both paths are distinct.

[3] On returning to the short lane end near Station Bridge, don't turn left but continue straight on to join the Catterick Garrison road just below St Mary's Church. Follow the road uphill and left into the Market Square. Ahead of you, at the side of Barclays Bank, is a narrow road. Take this and follow the upper path when the road goes down to the waterfalls. You will reach the Castle Walk, which takes you around the outside of the Norman castle, with very fine views down to the

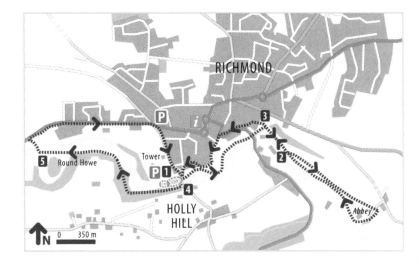

river. This in turn rejoins the Market Square at the top of New Rd. To quickly return to the car park, go down New Rd to Bargate and back to the Green.

4   Our walk continues from the bottom of Bargate and crosses Richmond Bridge. Turn right through a wide gate and follow the track for 100yds to where a low level path at the water's edge continues for almost ¼ mile to the bend in the river. From here the paths re-unite and continue well-defined to Round Howe.

5   There is a footbridge crossing the Swale to the Round Howe car park. Follow the footpath through the caravan site and onto Reeth Rd, passing the Convent on your right. At the top of Reeth Rd you will see an interesting yellow plaque on the wall of a building on your left: it marks the line of totality of the 1927 solar eclipse. From here, continue straight ahead downhill to the car park.

Points of interest

Easby Abbey was founded in 1152 and was actually run by canons who wore white rather than brown robes. The Premonstratensians were exempt from episcopal discipline and undertook both preaching and pastoral work. The abbey was sacked by Henry VIII in the 1530s and fell into disrepair.

Upper Washburn Valley

START Thruscross Reservoir car park, HG3 4BB (nearby), GR SE154574

DISTANCE 5 miles (8km)

SUMMARY Easy; good paths

MAPS OS Explorer 297 Lower Wharfedale and Washburn Valley; OS Landranger 104 Leeds & Bradford

WHERE TO EAT AND DRINK
The Stone House Inn, Thruscross (T01943-880325)

A straightforward walk, visiting the partly submerged remains of what was once a thriving, water-powered textile-manufacturing community.

[1] From the car park at the west end of the dam, cross the road and go through the gate opposite onto a permissive path. The path heads towards the reservoir, then follows the woodland edge near the water. At the first large inlet, turn left for a few yards along the former road, then right down a flight of steps to a footbridge. The path returns to the reservoir and proceeds north-west, but on reaching another former road you again turn left, then right, to regain the water's edge. Approaching the next inlet, follow the waymarks left through the wood, then right down steps to another bridge. The path now skirts the western arm of the reservoir, fed by Capelshaw Beck, and on reaching yet another drowned road you make the usual left then right turn off the road, following the waymarks. A little further along, you will reach the substantial ruins of Little Mill, which had two 18ft waterwheels. The path follows the watercourse which fed them: you can see the dam in this case by crossing the stile onto the road and following it right to the bridge which is built on it.

[2] Climb the hill beyond and turn right for Scaife Hill. Pass in front of the house, go through the left-hand gate, and take a straight line across three fields to a stile at the north-west corner of Whit Moor House. Keep to the north side of this farm, then go straight ahead to find the ruins of stoutly built Holme Field Head. Turn left here and walk for nearly a mile, first along the edge of the wood, then descending gently to cross a footbridge under Libishaw Scar.

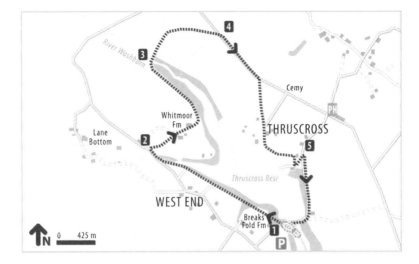

3 Turn right after crossing the stream and follow it down to a stile on the left where the wood begins. The stile leads to a narrow valley which you ascend, keeping well up on the left-hand side when there is no clear path. At the head of the little valley turn right, keeping above the marshy area, then make for the left-hand end of the ridge some distance away.

4 Emerge onto the road, either through the gate or over the stile 150yds further on. From the stile, turn right along the road for 500yds, leaving it, right, when approaching a dip in the road, over a stile by a gate. Follow the left-hand wall and at the next gate turn half-left to another gate, where you continue in the same direction to a stile. Aim now for the left-hand side of the barn ahead, where you pass through a gate and turn left to the road-end at Thruscross Green.

5 Head due south across the Green to find a stile. Cross and continue in the same line until the ground starts to fall. Follow the left-hand wall here as it turns left, descending gently. Keep just below the wall and, later, the hedge, but turn right just before a stone building to a gate by the Sailing Club. As you emerge onto the Club's private road turn left, then fork right along a grassy track, which brings you to the public road. Turn right and follow the road back to the dam, or, by going left for nearly ½ mile, to the Stone House Inn.

Around West Burton

START West Burton village
green, DL8 4JY, GR SE017867

DISTANCE 5 miles (8km)

SUMMARY Easy walking up a gradual
incline with a short, steep descent

MAPS OS Explorer OL30
Yorkshire Dales: Northern and
Central Areas; OS Landranger 98
Wensleydale & Upper Wharfedale

WHERE TO EAT AND DRINK
Fox & Hounds in West Burton
(T01969-663111): meals at lunch &
evening, children & dogs welcome

A short walk with splendid views across Wensleydale and full of interest – just
like a walk through history.

[1] From Burton Bridge, where Walden Beck emerges from a rocky
gorge, follow the walled lane past Flanders Hall and Howrane Farm to
Morpeth Gate ('gate' being the dialect for road), once the main road
from Middleham to Askrigg. After ½ mile note a finger post to the
Templars' Chapel on the left by a tubular steel gate. Go through the gate,
and the sheepfold beyond, and go forward into a long, narrow pasture.
Proceed along the hillside past a water trough, near the bottom wall, on
a narrow, grass-covered track. Where the track divides, take the right
branch up the hill to a gate with stone posts. Go through and forward
across four pastures with firstly a fence and then a wall on your left.
Bolton Castle can be seen across the dale. Go over a stile with a lambing
gate to a lane. Another stile now leads to the Templars' Chapel.

[2] From the lane strike diagonally south-east across the pasture to
an iron gate in the high corner between two plantations. Go through
the gate to the concrete road, which forms the top end of Hargill La.
Note the packhorse tracks, the old limestone quarries and a lime kiln.
Continue up the road, pausing at the top to take in the view. Push on
up to the ruined building where the drystone enclosure walls come
together to form a lane. Go forward to rejoin Morpeth Gate.

[3] Turning right, follow the green road for ½ mile to join the
Accommodation Rd at Morpeth Scar.

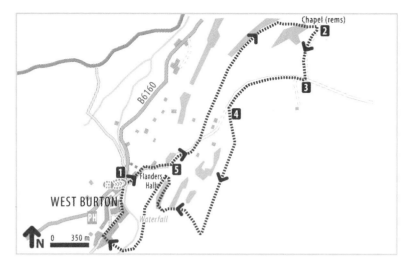

[4] Follow the rough stony track up to the left. Go forward along a walled lane through a gate to an open pasture, Burton Moor. Go along a cart-track marked 'West Burton' across the next pasture. Ahead is the hidden valley of Walden. Strike downhill north-westerly, via a ranging post, to a stile in the wall below it, then proceed with care down a steep, zig-zag path through the remains of Jack Wood. Aysgarth can be seen across the dale. Go over a stile at the bottom and cross a narrow field to another stile. Turn left and follow the wire fence down to Barrack Wood. Go down to, and over, a step stile.

[5] The path now makes straight for West Burton. Go through a handgate to the left of the field barn. Go forward to another handgate in the wood below the waterfall. At the foot of the second field turn sharp left to a handgate. Go through, down a short, steep path to the packhorse bridge, and join Mill La up to West Burton.

Points of interest

The Knights Templar established a small monastery on Pen Hill, about AD 1200. Only the ruined chapel, Templars' Chapel, remains above ground.

Burton Leonard to Bishop Monkton

START The Green in Burton Leonard, HG3 3SG, GR SE328638

DISTANCE 5½ miles (9km)

SUMMARY Easy; pleasant walking along roads and paths

MAPS OS Explorer 299 Ripon & Boroughbridge; OS Landranger 99 Northallerton & Ripon

WHERE TO EAT AND DRINK The Royal Oak, Burton Leonard (T01765-677322); Hare & Hounds, Burton Leonard (T01765-677355); Masons Arms, Bishop Monkton (T01765-676631)

A straightforward walk through peaceful countryside on lanes and quiet roads.

[1] From the Green take the road east, past the post office and out of the village past the Hare and Hounds pub. Continue for ¼ mile to a crossroads. Cross the road and go down the lane past the 'No Through Road' sign. Moor Farm can now be seen ½ mile ahead at the bottom of the lane.

[2] On reaching the farm, skirt around to the right of the large green building and take the chalk stone road through a gate and down to the plantation approximately ¼ mile ahead. When nearing the plantation, ignore the gate and lane to the left and follow the lane straight ahead, through the gate into the plantation. After approximately 100yds, and after going through another gate, the lane ends into a field. Walk diagonally left across the field until Hol Beck is reached. Walk downstream to the bridge, cross over and go diagonally left to a stile over the fence. Go over the stile and up the field, with the hedge on your right, to Foster Flatts Farm. Skirt the farm on the right to reach the road to Roecliff Corner ¼ mile ahead.

[3] On reaching the main road, turn left towards Bishop Monkton. Follow the road for about 2½ miles into Bishop Monkton, with its two pubs and a stream running along the main street.

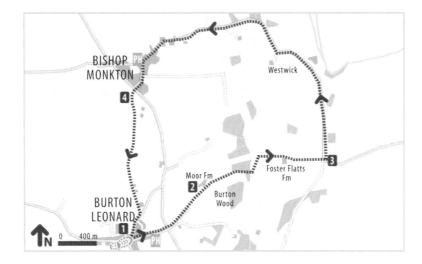

4 Follow the stream to the church and cross over the road into Church Farm. Keep left in the farmyard, with caravans on the right, and go over a stile. Keeping the hedge on the left, walk to the next stile. Go over and straight across the meadow to another stile in a hedge. Beyond this stile is a low bank: go up into a field. With the hedge again on the left, follow the edge of the field for 100yds to a stile in the corner, which can be missed if care is not taken. Go over the stile and across a ploughed, but well trodden, field to a stile into a meadow. When in the meadow head for the double-legged power pole. On reaching the pole, go through the gate behind and follow a lane to a large house surrounded by trees. Passing the house on your left, continue down the lane to its junction with Straight La. Turn right, pass St Cuthbert's Church on the right, and walk back to the Green.

Please note that all the stiles mentioned in the second part of the walk are marked with a large arrow, which can be seen from a considerable distance.

Burton Leonard to Brearton

START The Green in Burton
Leonard, HG3 3SG, GR SE328638

DISTANCE 5½ miles (9km)

SUMMARY Easy; pleasant
walking along roads and paths

MAPS OS Explorer 299 Ripon &
Boroughbridge; OS Landranger
99 Northallerton & Ripon

WHERE TO EAT AND DRINK
The Royal Oak, Burton Leonard
(T01765-677322);
Hare & Hounds, Burton Leonard
(T01765-677355);
The Malt Shovel, Brearton
(T01423-862929)

An interesting and quiet walk that visits two cracking villages and passes along some good lanes.

[1] From the Green take the west road out of the village, past the telephone box and up the hill alongside the Top Green. Half-way up the hill turn left across the Green and into Scara La, past Meadow Court and Flats House. Just beyond this point turn right into Lime Kilns La.

[2] About ¼ mile further on the lane splits: take the left fork past the nature reserve and down to the Lime Kilns Beck. Cross the footbridge and take the track rising to a gate and the junction with Riggs La. Turn right into the lane and continue uphill past a wood on the left to a gate at the top of the hill. Go through the gate and down the bridle path to Brearton village. On nearing the village, the track meets Lillygate La and splits two ways: the left fork continues the walk, the right is slightly further but does take in the village. Assuming the right turn is made, follow the lane to its junction with the main (only) street opposite the Malt Shovel. Turn left to the village green and pond, passing to the left of the Green along the lane to its junction with Lillygate La once more.

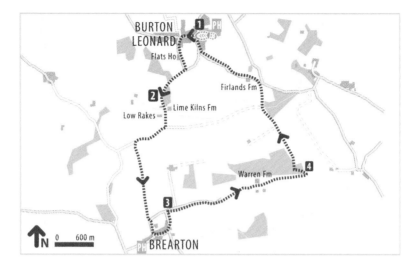

③ Follow the tarmac road to the right, past the gate to Hill Top Farm on the left, and on for approximately 1 mile. At a renovated farm on the left the lane then runs out to a grass track beyond a white double gate. Go through the gate and straight across the field, keeping a wood on the left and telephone poles on the right, to a wicket gate.

④ Beyond the gate turn sharp left and up a steep and sometimes slippery slope with a stone wall on the left and a wood on the right. Eventually the narrow track widens out to a bridle path and starts to fall downhill. You will come to Jonty Beck, and a bridge over it. At this point Riggs La joins from the left. Cross the bridge and go up the lane on the other side to the Toll House, which stands at the old turnpike point. Turn left past Firlands Farm and go back to Burton Leonard past the Royal Oak.

Marske to Skelton Moor

START Near the post office,
Marske, DL11 7LT, GR NZ105006

DISTANCE 5½ miles (9km)

SUMMARY Moderate; most of the
walk is on farm tracks, some paths

MAPS OS Explorer OL30
Yorkshire Dales: Northern and
Central Areas; OS Landranger 92
Barnard Castle & Richmond

WHERE TO EAT AND DRINK There
is a tea shop that sometimes opens
in Marske, next to the post office

A fine walk up Marske Beck, returning over Skelton Moor – quieter than many
walks in Swaledale.

1️⃣   From the post office walk along the small row of houses that
incorporates the old school, whose sundial is engraved Tempus Fugit.
Go through a gate with a yellow waymark, heading for Clints. The
track crosses a cattle grid and passes the Marske Methodist Church as
it heads down into beautiful old woodland. You can smell wild garlic
in places. As you come out of the woodland area, there is a fork in
the track. Take the left fork, continuing through the woods and then
between two fences up onto open ground. Continue to Orgate Farm
where the concrete track splits in two – one going into the farm and
the other down to Orgate Bridge.

2️⃣   Take neither of them and instead follow a grassy pathway
between the two, keeping downhill of the farm. Once past the farm,
go up through a gate and keep the field walls on your left until they
end. At this point, do not go uphill, but follow various small paths
until you are down by the Marske Beck at a recently restored pack
bridge, a beautiful spot.

3️⃣   Cross the pack bridge and turn left through a gate. Go right to
walk through the farmer's field. Grass is a crop to the farmer so walk
in single file up to the track, where you turn right. Follow the track
uphill, past Telfit Farm, through fields until you are out on the open

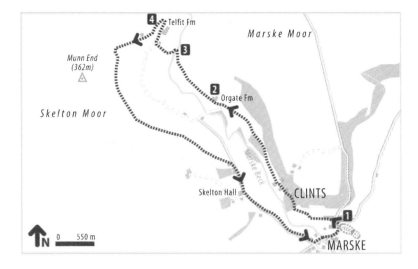

moorland of Skelton Moor. Follow the track across the moor to the corner of the field at a gate, where you will find an old stone gatepost lying down (it makes a grand seat!).

4 Do not go through the gate but instead turn left, heading east again along the fence and looking towards Hutton's Monument, the obelisk on the skyline. Follow the boundary path. It is joined on the left by another track and then goes through a gate. Be prepared, as you come over the rise, for a spectacular view of Clints Scar and the valley in which you walked earlier. Follow the track down to a road, where you turn right and walk down past Skelton Farm with wild aniseed growing in the hedges. At the end of the road turn left into Marske, go over the bridge and up the hill to the post office.

Points of interest

Marske is a beautiful village, with sundials on several houses. At the bridge, there is a tiny gap in the wall and steps leading down to the Beck.

Coverham Abbey

START Middleham market
place, DL8 4NP, GR SE127877

DISTANCE 6 miles (10km)

SUMMARY Easy

MAPS OS Explorer OL30 Yorkshire
Dales: Northern and Central Areas; OS
Landranger 99 Northallerton & Ripon

WHERE TO EAT AND DRINK
Richard III (T01969-623240);
Black Swan (T01969-622221)

A straightforward walk, with many points of interest. Some paths have been
diverted and are not as shown by the Ordnance Survey.

[1]   From the Richard III hotel, pass through the arch alongside and
up the yard beyond, turning right at the top. Turn left along the east
side of the castle, then right at the stile by the bungalow. Go straight
across the field and through the gate in the left-hand fence, climbing
the steep mound of the original Middleham Castle to reach the best
viewpoint for the present castle (once the home of Richard III). On
leaving the mound, follow the left-hand fence northwards towards
the road, but turn left over the stile just before reaching it. The path
follows the road; at a small clump of trees cross a stile, right, to
emerge onto the common. Turn left over another stile and follow the
field boundary on the left, parallel to the road. About 1 mile from
Middleham, and just past the pool, turn left through the gate at a
footpath signpost and turn right, parallel to the road but behind the
hedge. Cross two stiles, go through a hedge gap and two gates, to
reach the road at the entrance to Coverham Abbey Farm.

[2]   Turn left down the farm drive and right at the crossways at the
bottom, by the abbey ruins. Part of the abbey church is still standing
in the garden of Garth Cottage. Continue along the track, under the
arch of the former abbey gatehouse, turning right through a wicket
gate just before the house and climbing past a small waterfall into the
churchyard. Leave the churchyard by the north gate, turning left along
the main road towards Carlton. Follow it for 200yds before turning
left, across a stream and a stile. Go right, following the stream side to
emerge on a farm drive.

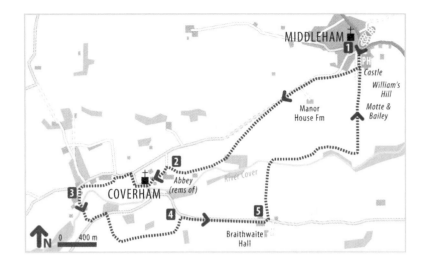

3️⃣ Turn left here, then left again in a few yards by the cottage, to descend an overgrown track to the footbridge at Bird Ridding Wath. Cross the bridge and follow the hedged path up to the road, where you turn left. Go right through the first gate and follow the left-hand fence up to its continuation by a line of old beeches, leading to a cross wall. For a better view, turn right for 40yds, cross the stile and climb straight up the field beyond to cross the wooden fence at the top.

4️⃣ Turn left and follow the field edge through a gate and over a stile, turning right through the next gate, then left to follow the field boundary down to a wicket gate into Hanghow La. Turn right along the lane for ¾ mile, then 5️⃣ left down the bridleway opposite Braithwaite Hall. Go straight ahead after the second gate, then swing right down to the bridge. After crossing the River Cover, turn right to pick up a clear track which climbs the bank, and continue in the same line across the field above. Pass through the hedge and turn left to the gate by the barn. Turn half-right and head for the middle of three barns visible ahead, but turn left at the fence to pass the left-hand barn. Go through the gate and turn left for Middleham.

Hebden Beck & Grassington

START Hebden, BD23 5DE, GR
SE025632 (park on the south
side of the B6265 at Hebden;
cross at the Clarendon Inn)

DISTANCE 6 miles (10 km)

SUMMARY Moderate

MAPS OS Explorer OL2 Yorkshire
Dales: Southern and Western
Areas; OS Landranger 98
Wensleydale & Upper Wharfedale

WHERE TO EAT AND DRINK
The Clarendon Hotel in Hebden is
a typical Yorkshire country inn with
good food and beer, while there is
lots more choice in Grassington

This is a lovely walk, investigating the old mine workings and walking along
Hebden Beck before an exploration of the pretty town of Grassington.

① Walking along the track through the old lead mines is
straightforward. However, there are many ruins and abandoned
workings. Cross the B6265 and go up the lane beside Hebden Beck.
The tall building on the left was once a cotton mill. As you go up the
lane, Nanny Spout waterfall can be glimpsed off to the right. Go past
cottages and over a packhorse bridge. The lane now becomes a track;
continue to the site of the loading yard where you can see the remains
of setts, or paving. Ford the stream at its shallowest point and continue
upstream. Dippers can be seen hereabouts. The hillocks to the left
are spoil heaps, thinly covered with grass, and the track winds round
them to the hilltop. On the skyline can be seen the smelting chimney.
Follow the track past bell pits to a clump of trees and cottages.

② This is Yarnbury, and there are now holiday cottages where once
there were the mine manager's home and office, and a row of houses
for other officials. The building to the right was the blacksmith's shop,
and in the grounds are the remains of the gunpowder store. Turn
left and go down the steep land to Grassington. After exploring the
delightful village of Grassington return up Main St to the Town Hall
and Devonshire Institute.

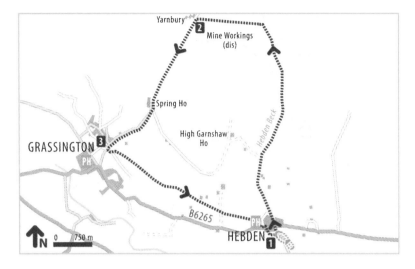

3️⃣   Turn right, then take the first turning left into High La. Pause to look back at Grassington's roofscape. You are now in a green lane, which can be muddy. Herb Robert grows in the cracks of the drystone walls. Continue along the lane, which later becomes a path, with stiles. When the old Grassington Hospital is reached, the path continues across the lawn in front of it to a gap in the wall. Beyond it, descend gently over fields and stiles to a lane, and onto the B6265. Cross the road and go down to the crossroads and your starting point.

Points of interest

Grassington was once the centre of the lead mining industry. It has many interesting folds, or yards. There is a National Parks Centre, and a variety of shops, inns and eating places. The Congregational Church was built in 1812.

At the centre of the lead mines is a 131ft/40m-high chimney, probably the most eye-catching in the Dales. There is also an old building which used to house a giant waterwheel.

32
33

Holgate Pastures

START Holgate, DL11 7EG, GR
SE073042 (ample parking on
the minor road from Newsham
to Marske at the crossroads)

DISTANCE Short route 6 miles (10km);
long route 9¾ miles (15.5km)

SUMMARY Moderate

MAPS OS Explorer OL30
Yorkshire Dales: Northern and
Central Areas; OS Landranger 92
Barnard Castle & Richmond

WHERE TO EAT AND DRINK
The closest places to eat and drink
are in Swaledale at either Reeth or
Richmond, about 5 miles distant

A high level walk across the moors of the Northern Dales, with spectacular views and an interesting history lesson on the old lead mine workings.

[1] Take the road signposted to Hurst, heading south-west. Do not go into Holgate Farm, but continue down into the stream valley with a ford and footbridge – an excellent place for a very early lunch! Cross the stream and continue on the track between two walls. Go through a gate to where the track becomes a metalled road again.

[2] Walk through the hamlets of Washfold and Hurst, noticing the old chimneys on the left, and continue (when the metalling stops) to follow a well-defined track through the old mining remains. Lots of minerals (quartz and galena to name but two) are to be found in this area. Some excellent grouse butts will be seen but resist the temptation to stop for lunch (if you have not already done so!) for as you come over the rise towards the National Park boundary, you will see the most glorious views over Arkengarthdale (to the north), Calver Hill (ahead) and Gibbon Hill (south).

[3] Do not go through the stone wall which marks the boundary, but turn left and walk along it on a well-trodden path for about 1¼ miles. The views are to the east now towards Marske and Helwith.

[4] You will come to a wall and, after going through the gate/opening in the wall, follow the track which heads diagonally away to the left

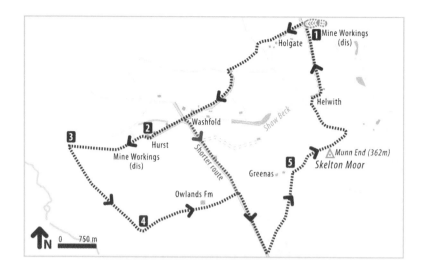

towards Owlands Farm. There, turn right and go down to the metalled road. At the road turn right and walk for about ½ mile until you see a road on the left signposted for Greenas Farm.

⑤ Take it and walk down to where it ends at three gates. Take one of the gates, turn right and head diagonally across the field on a track. On the left is a particularly spectacular view of Shaw Beck and Shaw Tongue; you should be able to pick out where you have been and be able to see your car. The track bears round to the left down the hill. Follow it down to the Shaw Beck at Helwith, where you will find a ford and footbridge. The track then becomes a metalled road, which you follow back up to your car.

The longer route is described above. To shorten it to 6 miles, turn left near the telephone box in Washfold and walk down to reach the road for Greenas Farm, continuing as described from there.

Points of interest

The area near Hurst was a mining area and is scattered with spoil heaps and old shafts and chimneys.

Keld & Ravenseat

START Keld, DL11 6LL, GR NY892011

DISTANCE 6 miles (10km)

SUMMARY Moderate walking
along field and fell paths,
with some road walking

MAPS OS Explorer OL30
Yorkshire Dales: Northern and
Central Areas; OS Landranger 98
Wensleydale & Upper Wharfedale

WHERE TO EAT AND DRINK
The Keld Lodge (T01748-886259)
offers food at lunchtime and in
the evening and is open all day

This is a walk into some wild moorland country. It can be exposed in bad
weather, but offers a real sense of freedom.

[1]   Leave the bottom end of Keld along Keld La, signposted 'Public
Footpath to Muker', and after ¼ mile, at a double Pennine Way sign,
go left, downhill, to the footbridge over the Swale. Here, detour
downstream for about 300yds to Kisdon Force, one of Swaledale's
finest waterfalls. Retrace your steps to the bridge. Cross the Swale and
continue uphill with East Gill Force on your right and turn left along a
path signposted 'East Stonesdale Farm'.

[2]   Turn left above the farm, going along a bridleway for ½ mile
through beautiful countryside with tantalising glimpses of Catrake
Force and Currack Force. When the Tan Hill road is reached, cross it,
go through a gate showing a footpath sign and walk along the top of
Cotterby Scar, following markers, for about ¾ mile. There are good
views of Wain Wath Force along this section. Where the scar ends, go
right along a farm road to empty Smithy Holme Farm.

[3]   There, go half-right across open moor, aiming for a 'Ravenseat–
Keld' signpost. Continue, passing on your right Eddy Fold, a large
sheepfold, guided by yellow markers, passing close to the edge of
Oven Mouth and Howe Edge ravines. Upstream of these two narrow
gorges the way descends pleasantly through pastures to the twin farms
of Ravenseat.

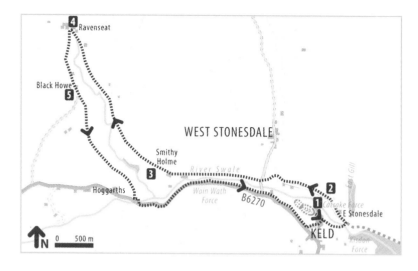

4 At the first house turn left along a track and cross an ancient packhorse bridge over Whitsundale Beck. Go up the road, past a house called Black Howe, ignoring a signpost saying 'Footpath to Hoggarth Bridge'.

5 Just beyond the house, go left by the moor wall. Go over a stile, passing two barns on your left, to cross another stile in the same wall. Go south-east on an undefined way down a boggy, rough pasture and then through a gap in a ruinous corner wall. Continue downhill, crossing a pasture, then a stile in the wall on your left. Go past another barn, over a waymarked stile and across another field to the B6270. Turn left along it, crossing the Swale at High Bridge, and continue along the road, with fine views of Wain Wath Force, Rainby Force and Currack Force, for the 1½ miles back to Keld.

Points of interest

Ravenseat is a former drover trading post, which used to have eleven households, a chapel and a pub.

Keld may be small but it is significant for long-distance walkers, as it is where the north/south Pennine Way meets the east/west Coast to Coast.

35 Nidderdale Way from Ramsgill

START The Lofthouse road,
Ramsgill, HG3 5RL, GR SE119710

DISTANCE 6 miles (10km)

SUMMARY Easy; good tracks and
paths along the Nidderdale Way

MAPS OS Explorer 298
Nidderdale; OS Landranger
99 Northallerton & Ripon

WHERE TO EAT AND DRINK
The Crown Hotel, Lofthouse
(T01423-755206) and the Yorke
Arms at Ramsgill (T01423-755243)

This walk visits the pretty villages of Lofthouse, Middlesmoor and Ramsgill in
Upper Nidderdale.

[1] Continue along the Lofthouse road, over the packhorse bridge,
then turn right on the lane signposted to Bouthwaite. Go up the lane,
noting the old station house on the right – a relic of the Nidderdale
Light Railway. At Bouthwaite, turn left on the footpath past Grange
Farm, once owned by Fountains Abbey. Follow the path on the field
track past the lower edge of a conifer plantation, then past the back of
a farm and down to the road.

[2] Cross the stiles at either side of the road. Follow the old railway
track, then go to the right across a field and through a beggar's stile to
the road. The old vicarage is on the hill in front of you. Cross the road
diagonally to the left, go over a stile and follow the path, which brings
you out at the back of the Crown Hotel, Lofthouse. Turn left through
the village. At the main road turn right, signposted Middlesmoor,
then, almost immediately, turn left over the little bridge across
Howstean Beck.

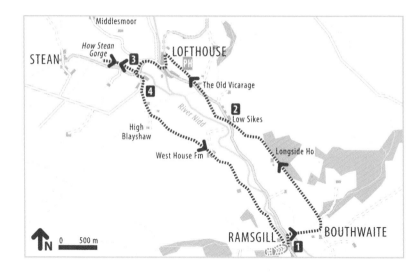

3 If you wish to extend your walk, turn right and walk up the lane for ½ mile to the entrance to How Stean Gorge. There is a café here, and toilets. The walk down the gorge (entrance fee) brings you out at a wicket gate just above the little bridge. To the left as you stand on the bridge, there is a rough lane which takes you past the caravan site, steeply uphill to cottages.

4 Take the next turn left, along a walled lane to a bridge. Just above are ruined buildings and a channel has been cut in the stream bed. Continue forward by field paths past Low West House. The path gradually descends and you return to Ramsgill through a farm yard.

Points of interest

The walk follows part of the Nidderdale Way, a long-distance footpath. In April the dale is at its best, with fresh greens and many lambs. In the centre of the village of Lofthouse is a fountain, the war memorial. Further up the road is a horse trough commemorating the Armistice.

Austwick & the Norber Erratics

START Austwick, LA2
8BB, GR SD767684

DISTANCE 6½ miles (10.5km)

SUMMARY Easy

MAPS OS Explorer OL2 Yorkshire
Dales: Southern and Western

Areas; OS Landranger 98
Wensleydale & Upper Wharfedale

WHERE TO EAT AND DRINK
The Game Cock Inn in Austwick
(T015242-51226) is the best choice,
although the many facilities of
Settle are only 5 miles away

An easy climb with fine views, incorporating a visit to the famous Norber Erratics.

[1] Leave Austwick by the Horton road and turn left after the school up Town Head La. Continue until a crossroad of tracks is reached and turn left for about 50yds.

[2] Take a stone stile on your right and follow the tractor path across the field to reach a gate in a stone wall. Turn right at the wall to follow the footpath for Norber running alongside the wall. At a cross wall go through a stone stile into a sheep gathering pen, leaving immediately by the left-hand wall corner. Keep the wall on your left and follow it as it curves round to your left. On seeing a large stone across the pathway take a path to the right that ascends to a plateau where a signpost to Crummack and Clapham will be seen. Follow the Crummack path, which rises to another plateau from where a path on the left takes you up to the Norber Erratics. From the stones a ladder stile in a wall corner to the north takes you onto the open moor. Immediately over the stile turn left and follow the wall for about 100yds until you see a path rising to your right. Take this path and follow it to the lowest point on the ridge, where you will meet a stone wall. Take the first path that follows the wall to the right and leads, in about a mile, to a stile onto a path coming up from Clapham.

[3] Turn right here to follow the path as it climbs to Long Scar and then down slightly to a junction of three paths. The other alternative gives by far the best views on a clear day: the path follows the cairns along the top of the limestone plateau until a path is reached before

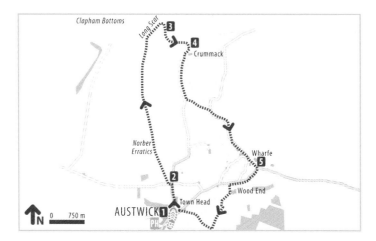

the last cairn. Turning right here brings you in a short while to the junction of the three paths. At this junction of paths from Crummack, Selside and Clapham, take the right-hand path running in a southerly direction towards Crummack.

(4) When the intake wall of Crummack Farm is reached, turn right and follow the footpath through two farm gates into Crummack La. Follow this lane until a similar lane, signposted to Wharfe, comes in from your left. Take this lane and follow it to Wharfe. On reaching a metalled road, turn left to pass through the hamlet of Wharfe.

(5) In a few hundred yards a more major road is reached. Turn right onto this road to the first farm track on your left, which is also a bridleway signposted 'Wood Lane'. Follow this track, turning right just before the farm buildings to reach a walled lane. Keep with the left-hand wall as the right-hand wall deserts the path. The right-hand wall returns to accompany the path onto the main road, ignoring a left-hand loop just before the main road. On the main road turn left to enter Austwick.

Points of interest

Norber Erratics translated actually means 'Boulders in the wrong place' and are remnants of Silurian stone left after the last ice age.

Clapham

START The National Park Centre car park, Clapham, LA2 5HH, GR SD745692

DISTANCE 6½ miles (10.5km)

SUMMARY Moderate

MAPS OS Explorer OL2 Yorkshire Dales: Southern and Western Areas; OS Landranger 98 Wensleydale & Upper Wharfedale

WHERE TO EAT AND DRINK
The New Inn in Clapham (T015242-51203) is an old coaching inn with a good range of beer and food

An upland walk along quiet tracks, with breathtaking views and many interesting geological features.

1 Turn right on leaving the car park, taking the road towards the church. Just before the church take the lane to your right, passing through two short, dark tunnels.

2 Take the first left turn and follow the walled lane. Ahead and to the right are Thwaite Scars, while the hill on your left is Ingleborough. Just over 1 mile along the lane you will see, below you and to the left, the entrance to Ingleborough Cave.

3 At the end of the lane follow a less distinct path half-right and cross the ladder stile. Approximately 100yds further on, the path bears left. As you reach a stretch of limestone pavement on your left the dramatic mass of Pen-y-Ghent appears ahead of you.

4 Another bridleway soon joins from the right. Turn along this, descend to Crummack Farm and follow the walled Crummack La.

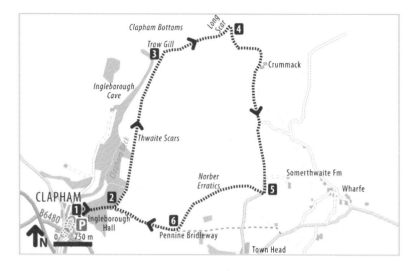

5   After 1½ miles take the path to your right, signposted Norber. Pass along the cliffs of Nappa Scars and, a little further on, to your right, you will see the Norber Erratics. After exploring them, return to the path and follow it past Robin Proctor's Scar. The path runs alongside a drystone wall and then diagonally across a field, passing a dried-up mere, to a ladder stile.

6   Turn right along another walled lane, which will take you back to your original path from Clapham. Retrace the outward route to the start.

Points of interest

The walk has wonderful views of two of Yorkshire's famous 'Three Peaks', Ingleborough at 2,372ft/723m, and Pen-y-Ghent at 2,277ft/694m. Clapham is a delightful village, with a pretty wooded beck running through it. The naturalist Reginald Farrar lived here, as did, reputedly, the 'Witch of Clapham'.

Richmond Beacon

START Nuns Close car park,
Richmond, DL10 4QB, GR NZ171010

DISTANCE 6½ miles (10.5km)

SUMMARY Moderate; there is
a long climb but the route and
terrain are straightforward

MAPS OS Explorer 304 Darlington
& Richmond; OS Landranger 92
Barnard Castle & Richmond

WHERE TO EAT AND DRINK
There is a large choice of cafés,
pubs and hotels in Richmond

The walk involves a long steady climb, but combines superb views with some
excellent walking along Whitcliffe Scar.

1 From the car park go left up Hurgill Rd and right into Quarry
Rd, climbing steeply. At a road junction continue straight ahead along
Racecourse Rd, and where the road bends left go straight ahead along
a signposted path and over a wall stile into Old Richmond Racecourse.

2 Turn left, passing the old stone Race Judge's Box. Beyond this, go
through a white gate to the Old Reeth Rd. Turn right along the road,
past High Gingerfield Lodge, and after ½ mile turn right just before
Beacon Cottage into unsigned Beacon La and continue for 2 miles
along Coalsgarth Edge. On the way, to your left, Richmond Beacon on
Beacon Hill is visible. A short detour of about ¾ mile along Beacon La
to the Beacon, on a public right of way, is worth taking. Having seen
the beacon from close quarters, return to Beacon La and continue
along it, north-west to Aske Beck. Cross on stepping stones and
immediately go through the facing wooden gate, beyond which the
track climbs for ¼ mile to a metal gate displaying blue waymarkers.

3 Do not go through this gate. Instead, follow the path on its left
to a white post marked with blue arrows, where you turn left along a
path southwards over Richmond Out Moor, with Beacon Plantation
on your left and twin radio masts ahead on the horizon. Re-cross Aske
Beck to reach two tall waymarker posts, which direct you over the
moor to exit through a gate to the Old Reach Rd. Turn right along it

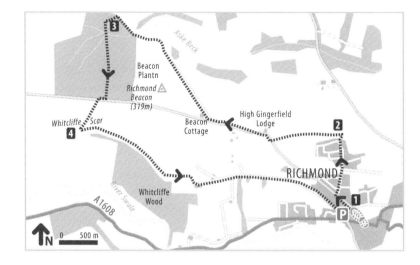

for 50yds to where a public footpath sign points you over a ladder stile in a wall. Now go half-right for a little way along a path which merges with a tractor track, before going south across rough pasture, aiming for the top of a monument seen peeping over a wall. Go through a small gate to the two remaining of three memorial stones set 24ft apart, marking Willance's Leap.

④   You are now on Whitcliffe Scar, from where there are panoramic views of Swaledale, distant Pen Hill in Wensleydale and Great Whernside. Go left along Whitcliffe Wood. Bear left at some gorse bushes to exit through an open gateway in a facing fence. Continue along a track which soon curves right down the hillside to a gated farm road opposite High Leases Farm. Turn left along it, passing Whitcliffe Farm on your left, and follow the surfaced road down Westfields for a mile to Richmond and the end of a good walk.

Points of interest

Richmond Beacon is an old signal station standing 1,045ft above sea level. It was lit when the Spanish Armada passed by.

Upper Dentdale

START The Sportsmans Inn car park, Cowgill Dent, LA10 5RG, GR SD768863 (please ask landlord's permission to park)

DISTANCE 6½ miles (10.5km)

SUMMARY Moderate, though if you tackle Great Knoutberry Hill in the mist it becomes difficult!

MAPS OS Explorer OL2 Yorkshire Dales: Southern and Western Areas; OS Landranger 98 Wensleydale & Upper Wharfedale

WHERE TO EAT AND DRINK
The Sportsmans Inn is on the route (T01539-625282), while there is a bigger choice 5 miles down the valley at Dent

Explore the history of this wonderful train line, its spectacular viaducts and the highest station in England.

① Turn right (uphill) from the car park of the Sportsman's Inn and follow the road for 400yds till it arrives at a sharp bend and a bridge. Cross the bridge (there is some parking here if the landlord does not let you park at his car park). A lane directly uphill passes through a few houses before opening up spectacularly as the Arten Viaduct is revealed. The size from this angle is amazing and there are some notice boards nearby describing the type of ore used in the area. The bridlepath climbs steeply till it passes under the viaduct and then follows the north side of Arten Gill. Arten Gill has formed a deep v-shaped valley, which was what made the viaduct necessary in the first place. Follow the bridleway for nearly a mile until you are just short of the col. A long-distance footpath (the Pennine Journey) crosses the bridleway at this point.

② Turn left onto it and cross a stile onto the open hillside. The path skirts the high ground of Great Knoutberry Hill and contours in a northerly direction for nearly 1½ miles till it turns into a track and soon meets the tarmac road from Garsdale. If you are tempted to try and climb Great Knoutberry, it is possible but the land is featureless (particularly after the summit) and hard underfoot; stick to the path if possible.

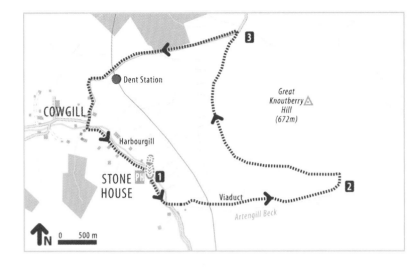

3 On arriving at the Garsdale Rd turn left (downhill) and follow it past some plantations for 1 mile to Dent station, the highest station in England at 1,150ft (also one of the most attractive). It is possible to stay here in the bunk barn but it can be rather bleak in winter! Having explored the station, carry on down the now steep and winding road to Lea Yeat, just next to the small hamlet of Cowgate at the foot of Dentdale. Turn right and follow the embryonic River Dee for ½ mile until you arrive back at the Sportsman's Inn.

Points of interest

 Dent Marble was once the most popular marble in the country, although it was in fact made out of dark limestone with a high fossil content.

Arden and Dent Head Viaducts are two of the most impressive in the country. Arten has eleven arches, is 117ft high and 20yds wide: a Victorian masterpiece.

START Blubberhouses, LS21 2NZ,
GR SE168553 (park at the foot of the
main A59 hill below Hopper Lane)

DISTANCE 7 miles (11km)

SUMMARY A straightforward,
interesting walk

MAPS OS Explorer 297 Lower
Wharfedale and Washburn Valley;
OS Landranger 104 Leeds & Bradford

WHERE TO EAT AND DRINK
The Hopper Lane Hotel
(T01943-880191) is at Blubberhouses;
in Fewston there is a vegetarian tea
shop which is well worth a visit

Passing two reservoirs, the walk is on good paths and covers woodland and
fields with far-reaching views.

1   Walk along and up the hill, on the main road towards Harrogate,
to Hopper La layby. At the top of the layby go over the stile into the
wood and follow the track, keeping to the right, down and along the
edge of the reservoir. Keep walking until you come to the end, by a
fence. Here, turn left through the gate into a wood. Go through the
wood to a minor road.

2   Turn right, passing the school on your left. A little way on, go
through the gap into the woodland on your right. Go through to
another minor road. Turn right, following the road over the Fewston
Embankment to the Swinsty Moor Plantation and National Trust car
park. Go through the wicket gate by the 'Public Footpath' sign, and
through the trees of Swinsty Moor Plantation, to arrive at ancient
Swinsty Hall.

3   Bearing right, follow the track up through the wood to a gate into
a field. Walk straight ahead, up two fields over stone stiles, then bear
slightly left across a field to a wooden stile. Follow the wall to a gate
with a wall stile near it. You will now enter a walled track; keep to the
right. Pass two lovely old 1683 and 1668 houses, and reach Timble.

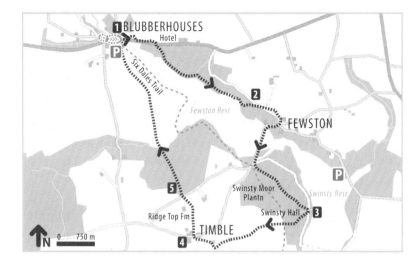

④ If you turn right, Timble Inn is just a short walk down the road, but the route follows the sign to Blubberhouses. At the sign go over the stile by the iron gate and walk ahead through a walled enclosure. Go straight up the field, through the gate on the right and down a field to a stile in the corner, with a wooden plank. Walk diagonally to the left over the next field to a gate to a minor road. Cross and enter the wood by the Blubberhouses sign.

⑤ Take the middle track through the wood. Keeping to the right, you will come to a track road. Go over this into a wood. Go down to a wooden bridge over a stream, then on to a stone stile. Walk ahead to enter a green lane; follow this and go over a fence stile. The track bears right, then left through gateposts to an iron gate stile. Make towards the trees to reach a stile in the wall. Keep on the left track through the field, with the wall on your right, and go over the stone stile by a tree. Now, with the wall on your left, go ahead over a wooden stile and keep left to a stone stile in the corner. Follow the wall to a wooden stile. Go over and down the fields, with the little church to your left, and over a stile back to your car.

41 Ilkley Moor

START The moorside road
south of the college in Ilkley,
LS29 8HL, GR SE130468

DISTANCE 7 miles (11km)

SUMMARY A moderate walk over
open moorland, with a touch of history

MAPS OS Explorer 297 Lower
Wharfedale and Washburn Valley;
OS Landranger 104 Leeds & Bradford

WHERE TO EAT AND DRINK
Many pubs and cafés in Ilkley

Ilkley Moor is an enticing area of high moorland, full of interest and history, with
good paths for walking – the difficulty being that there are so many!

①   From the nearby White Wells Museum car park, a path crossing
a stream with waterfalls leads up to the museum. Behind and a little
to the right of the museum, a track bears left, uphill, towards Ilkley
Crags. Occasionally steps help with the climb; ignore all small paths
off and tracks crossed. Cairns mark your route to a boundary stone,
Lanshaw Lad.

②   Soon after, the Twelve Apostles Stone Circle is reached on your
left. A boundary wall is soon visible ahead and, a little before it, a
not too clear footpath leads off to the left to reach the wall at a stile.
Alternatively, continue to the wall, cross a stile, and turn left by the
wall to the correct stile. A track now leads a little away from the wall,
downhill. Reach a fence on the opposite side of the wall and two stiles.
Cross the stile on the right to look at Horncliffe Well and the stones
around, then re-cross and use the stile on the left. A narrow footpath
soon takes you a few yards away from the fence but generally runs
parallel to it. Cross small streams with care. Continue along the clear
path through the heather, after passing the corner of the fence to reach
an old railway carriage.

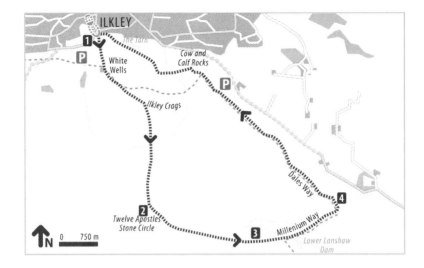

3   Cross a track and, slightly to the right, take the narrow path which leads down to pass to the left of Lower Lanshaw Dam, a small reservoir. Keep to the left of a boundary marker as you walk downhill. The path bears left and reaches a wider track. Turn left and soon fork right to cross the stream in the valley. Turn right, going steadily uphill along the main track after crossing, and walk downhill to a junction.

4   Turn left to follow a wallside track. You are now on the Ebor Way. Hangingstone Rd is soon below, but keep to the track just above the steeper part of the hillside. The Cow and Calf Hotel and rocks are visible ahead. Bear right along a narrower path downhill just before the hotel. Generally maintain direction towards the rocks, which disappear from view for a short distance: don't worry, most paths lead you to them. Descend to pass between the isolated Calf and the larger Cow. Continue slightly down to reach a wider track going uphill. Before reaching a fence, turn right along a path heading for the now visible Tarn. Soon the path crosses a valley with a footbridge over a stream. Reach the Tarn and continue along the surfaced track by its side and downhill towards houses. Turn left just before these up to a wooden shelter and then bear left downhill, across a footbridge, to the road and your car.

Malham Explorer

START National Park Centre car park as you approach Malham, BD23 4DA, GR SD901628

DISTANCE 7 miles (11km)

SUMMARY Medium difficulty walk unless you decide to tackle Gordale Scar, which would make it difficult

MAPS OS Explorer OL2; OS Landranger 98 Wensleydale & Upper Wharfedale

WHERE TO EAT AND DRINK
Malham has two country inns: the Buck Inn (T01729-830317) and the Listers Arms (T01729-830330)

Possibly the best known walk in the Dales, taking in Malham Cove, Janet's Foss, Malham Tarn and, if you want, Gordale Scar.

1 As you enter Malham village, there is a small stream on your right; cross this at a small bridge and double back away from the village on its east bank. After 200yds take a left-hand turn to Janet's Foss and follow a small stream through fields and into woodland. After a mile the waterfall of Janet's Foss is reached. From here, climb sharply up past the waterfall on the left of the road. At the ridge there is then a choice of route.

2 The easy and sensible route takes the path from the bridge left up the steepening hillside, which meets the road after ½ mile. Turn right and climb up the road for 1½ miles till it bends sharply at Street Gate, which is where you meet the second route option.

3 Cross the bridge and turn immediately left to follow the stream towards Gordale Scar. The steep hillside encroaches until you are in a tight valley and when the path finishes you have to climb a steep slab of rock called Gordale Scar. This is challenging and unless you are confident scrambling up rocks, avoid this route. After the initial climb a path appears next to the stream and carries on up the gorge until it breaks out onto a series of limestone pavements.

4 The path crosses a wall and joins the easier route just short of the left turn. Follow the road for a further ½ mile till you come to a

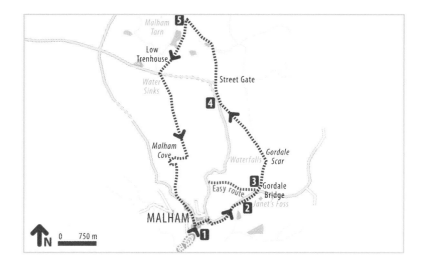

stream with some parking on the right. To see Malham Tarn walk through the cars and take the path for 200yds and there is a good view of the tarn. Return to the car park.

⑤　Immediately after crossing the bridge, turn left and follow the west bank of the river. You are now following the Pennine Way to Malham Cove. The 1½-mile path passes a point called Water Sinks, where the stream disappears underground to re-emerge near the foot of Malham Cove through a series of underground caves. On reaching the limestone pavements at the top of Malham Cove, cross over to the west-hand side, following the steep but clearly marked and protected path to its foot and the return of the river. Climbers are often showing their skills on Malham Cove's vast amphitheatre and are worth a watch. The route back to Malham is now obvious on a wide track that keeps to the river until it soon meets the road 200yds from the centre of Malham village.

Points of interest

Standing 300ft high and 900ft wide, Malham Cove is a vast amphitheatre of carboniferous limestone, featuring recently in the latest Harry Potter film.

Shaw Mills to Ripley

START Shaw Mills, HG3 3HU,
GR SE258625 (park on the roadside)

DISTANCE 7 miles (11km)

SUMMARY Easy/moderate

MAPS OS Explorer 298
Nidderdale; OS Landranger
99 Northallerton & Ripon

WHERE TO EAT AND DRINK
There are excellent tearooms at
Ripley Castle (T01423-770152)

A fine walk following a section of the Nidderdale Way towards Ripley and its
famous castle, before a pleasant return along some quiet lanes.

1️⃣ From the roadside walk along the road towards Ripon. At the last
house in the village the road turns sharp left; leave the road and cross
over three stiles, very close together, into a field. Walk across the field
to a five-barred gate and a Nidderdale Way sign. Go through the gate,
turn half-left and climb diagonally up the field, to a stone wall and
another Nidderdale Way sign. Turn right and, with the wall on your
left, walk down towards marshy ground. The track rises sharply to
farm buildings at the top of the hill. Turn right at the farm and follow
the track down through a single gate to Kettle Spring Farm. Pass to the
right of the buildings and out onto the farm lane. Follow the lane to its
junction with the main road.

2️⃣ Turn left up the road for ½ mile past a house in a wood and then
turn right at the Nidderdale Way sign into a lane with a plantation on
the left. Walk along the lane and down a single path with a plantation
on the right, to stepping stones over Cayton Beck.

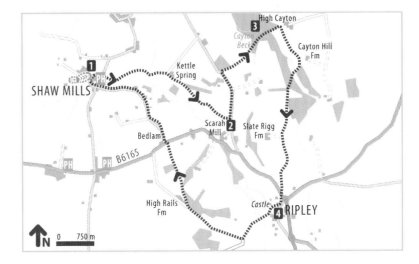

3   Cross the stones and pass through the gate on the right into the
glen. Turn left and, with the fence of the wood on the left and marshy
ground on the right, walk for ½ mile. There are several arrows on
posts indicating the way to a gate in a stone wall. Pass through the
gate and follow the edge of the wood on the right down past a small
red brick building. Go through a gate and down the field. Go over an
arched bridge and left to a gate into a wood. The path from the gate
is narrow and can be very slippery after rain. Climb the path through
the wood, following Nidderdale Way signs into Braithwaite La and
down across the B6165 into Ripley.

4   From Ripley walk past the Castle and into Hollybank La. Go
uphill, following a park wall. When the wall turns right, we leave the
Nidderdale Way, which carries on into the wood. Continue to follow
the wall. Go over a stile, through a gate and over another stile. After
this second stile the path veers away to the left. Leaving the wall to
the right, cross the field diagonally to a post with an arrow. Follow the
fence down over two gates. The main road can now be seen; follow
the hedge on your right, passing through the side garden of a recently
renovated house and onto the road. Cross the road, known as Whipley
Bank, and go into Law La. From here it is 1 mile of pleasant walking
down to Shaw Mills.

Settle to Stainforth

START Settle, public car park
just south-west of the market
place, BD24 9DW, GR SD819637

DISTANCE 7 miles (11km)

SUMMARY A medium-graded
walk over mixed terrain, with some
moorland walking on paths

MAPS OS Explorer OL2 Yorkshire
Dales: Southern & Western Areas;
OS Landranger 98 Wensleydale
& Upper Wharfedale

WHERE TO EAT AND DRINK
The 'Old Naked Man' Café
(T07292-32030) or the Lion Inn
(T01729-822203), both in Settle

The area near Settle has many historical features of interest, with pretty villages
set amidst lovely scenery of rolling hills and limestone scars.

1 From the market square head up the lane steeply past the Co-op.
After 100yds the road bends left and then heads along the outskirts of
the village till it eventually comes out at the main Horton road. After
100yds turn into the pretty village of Langcliffe with its old church and
splendid Yorkshire stone houses.

2 After arriving at the village hall, turn left past the kennels and
take the footpath across two fields heading towards the railway line.
After walking next to the railway line, you soon come across an
excellent example of an old lime kiln. It is free to go in and have a
look round. The path carries on alongside the railway for another
½ mile, and when it bends west the path carries on across a field and
soon arrives at a stile and the main road. Walk alongside the road for
a further 100yds before turning off and heading into the village of
Stainforth. There is plenty to see in Stainforth and it is a lovely village,
but head for the stepping stones over the river and cross to the lane
heading east past some attractive cottages.

3 The lane is signposted to Catrigg Force and climbs steeply up
the hillside, with the river clearly to your left. After ¾ mile there is
a signpost to the left, which drops down to a great viewing point for
Catrigg Force, well worth the short detour.

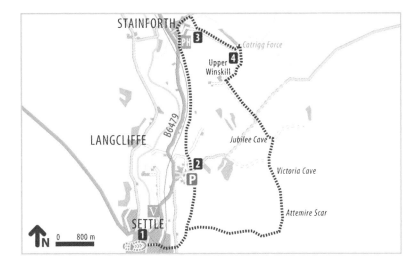

④ Follow the lane as it bends to the right and, after arriving at Upper Winskill Farm, turn left till you reach the quiet road leading from Settle to Malham Tarn. Cross the road next to a cattle grid and then head initially down then up a green path. Cross a stile, then you'll reach a lane and gate. Head directly on, passing under Victoria Cave and with a steep hillside on the left. After another ½ mile the path divides; turn right and follow the path under the dramatic Attermire Scar. The path gradually climbs from the intersection of paths and at the top, in a gap in the hills, the views open up and Settle can be seen far below. It is a steep but satisfying descent towards Settle, joining a green lane halfway down.

Points of interest

Discovered only 150 years ago, Victoria Cave may have existed over 100,000 years earlier as remains of hippos, elephants and hyenas were discovered, dating from before the last ice age.

There are two famous waterfalls in Stainforth: the first is Catrigg Force, but it is worth discovering the excellent Stainforth Falls just below the village.

START Dent, car park at the west end of village, LA10 5QL, GR SD704870

DISTANCE 7½ miles (12km)

SUMMARY A fine upland walk with a steep but straightforward climb

MAPS OS Explorer OL2 Yorkshire Dales: Southern & Western Areas; OS Landranger 98 Wensleydale & Upper Wharfedale

WHERE TO EAT AND DRINK
Plenty of choice in Dent

One of the easier routes to obtain some genuinely remote countryside and moorland; not many people tread here.

1 Leave the car park and cross the main road to a lane opposite. Follow it to a green area and pass this, following the lane past some delightful whitewashed cottages. The lane leads to a stony path, which heads up Flinter Gill. Follow this steep track to a gate. Pass through and continue heading upward. Eventually the track leads to a gate, which marks the beginning of the moorland; the track also becomes walled at this point. Walk up the walled track to meet a similar track running across it (this old road runs from Barbondale Rd to Ingleton).

2 Turn left at this junction to follow the old road. The fine views over Dentdale make this walk along the lane a worthwhile journey, despite the varying conditions underfoot.

3 When a track is reached running up from Deepdale, keep with the right-hand track as it heads upwards on a high-level traverse of Deepdale. When you are opposite the waterfalls of Gastack Beck at the head of Deepdale, look for a small wooden gate in the wall on your right, approximately 100yds before a metal gate across the track. Go through this gate and head half-left (south-west) across the moor to reach a stone wall. Follow the wall up onto the ridge to meet a cross wall running along the top of the ridge. Turn right at this wall to follow it as it rises to Gatty Pike, noticing on the way the large County Stone situated where the wall running up from Long Gill joins the ridge wall. From the cairn on Gatty Pike there are excellent views of Whernside, just across the valley, and of Ingleborough to the

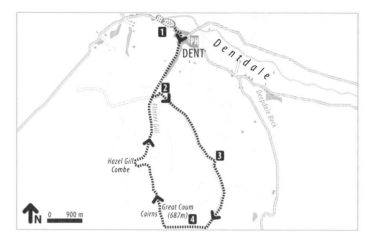

right. From Gatty Pike continue following the ridge wall, crossing an incoming wall from the right and a small rocky outcrop. The wall reaches a corner created by its right-angled turn left and a wall running from the right. Negotiate the wall, which has no stile, and turn left to follow the original wall once more.

4 After about 100yds you will need to negotiate another junction of walls to reach the summit cairn of Great Coum. Leave the summit to rejoin the wall previously crossed. Turn left to follow the wall descending the moor. Cross an incoming wall from the left and continue with the wall as it further descends the moor. When it turns to the left to head in a northerly direction, keep with it. When it turns once more to descend the moor more steeply, leave its confines to head in the same direction (north) across the moor to reach the Megger Stones. From the Megger Stones head northwards down the moor to locate a wall corner. Follow the right-hand wall down to the walled track and turn left to retrace your way back to Dent via Flinter Gill.

Points of interest

Great Coum is the highest point of the walk at 2,250ft/686m. From the summit there are extensive views of the Lakeland skyline to the north-west and of the closer Howgills to the north. Megger Stones is an area of scree, onto which many cairns have been built.

46

47

Bainbridge & Semer Water

START Bainbridge village green,
DL8 3EE, GR SD935904

DISTANCE 7½ miles (12km);
shorter version 6½ miles (10.5km)

SUMMARY A moderate walk, with
a steady climb along a Roman
road and a steep descent to
Semer Water (the south end of
Semer Water can be very wet)

MAPS OS Explorer OL30 Yorkshire
Dales: Northern & Central Areas;
OS Landranger 98 Wensleydale
& Upper Wharfedale

WHERE TO EAT AND DRINK
The Corn Mill Tea Room
(T01969-650212) has excellent
sandwiches; Rose & Crown
Hotel (T01969-650735)

Semer Water is the second largest natural stretch of water in North Yorkshire
(after Malham Tarn) and the walk brings this out to great effect.

1   From the village green follow the road signposted for Burtersett,
Semer Water and Marsett for ½ mile. When the road bends to the left,
take the walled green lane ahead – the Roman Cam High Rd. Follow
this through glorious Wensleydale scenery for just over 2 miles.

2   As you pass Green Scar, take the path to your left, signposted
'Marsett'. The path goes through a gate and runs alongside a small
area of limestone scar and a derelict drystone wall. Ignoring the more
obvious green path going off to your right, make for the ladder stile
half-left and follow the path to the bottom of the hill. Take the metalled
track left through a gate and onto the main road. If you wish to avoid
the boggy section of the walk, turn left along the road and follow it as
far as Semer Water Bridge. Otherwise, turn right into Marsett.

3   Go left after crossing the bridge and left again along the footpath
marked Semer Water and Stalling Busk. Ahead of you is the flat-
topped hill of Addlebrough. Cross the footbridge and summon all
your resourcefulness and athleticism to get you from one dry patch to
another along the next few yards of the path. Another footbridge, to
your left, takes you across the next stream. Over this bridge the path

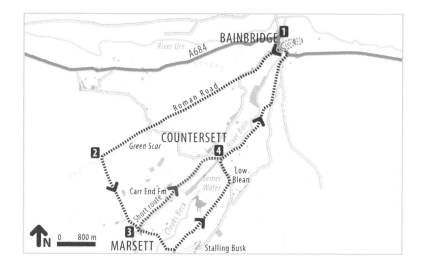

goes left alongside a wall. After 50yds go through the gap in the wall and continue left across a boggy field. Just past the small stone barn, cross the stile to your left. The worst of the mud is now behind you. Continue straight ahead past a ruined church and along the banks of Semer Water. Cross the ladder stile onto the main road and follow it left past the Carlow and Mermaid's Stones to Semer Water Bridge.

④   Take the footpath to your right (or left for those who have taken the shorter route option) signposted 'Bainbridge' and follow the banks of the River Bain, said to be the shortest river in England. When the path becomes indistinct after leaving the bank and crossing a ladder stile, make for the narrow gap in the wall ahead of you. From the top of the hill the lovely view of Askrigg is one familiar to anyone who has watched *All Creatures Great and Small*. On reaching the road, turn left and follow it back to Bainbridge.

Points of interest

From the first to the fourth centuries Bainbridge was an important Roman town and the site of a fort. The village has many reminders of the past, including the stocks on the village green and the tradition of horn-blowing, which dates back to when it stood at the edge of the forest of Wensleydale.

48 Buckden Pike

START Buckden, car park towards the north side of village, BD23 5JA, GR SD942773

DISTANCE 7½ miles (12km)

SUMMARY Difficult; a steep climb up one of the best mountains in the Yorkshire Dales, with lovely views and generally good paths

MAPS OS Explorer OL30 Yorkshire Dales: Northern & Central Areas; OS Landranger 98 Wensleydale & Upper Wharfedale

WHERE TO EAT AND DRINK
There is a tea shop in Buckden, but most people end up in the Buck Inn (T01729-830317)

[1]   From the car park at Buckden, go through the gate and follow the stony track up Buckden Rakes. This was once the main road over to Wensleydale. The track goes through Rakes Wood, and in spring creamy tassels of bird cherry overhang it. At the corner, pause to look at the view west to Hubberholme.

[2]   The track curves to the right and up to a gate. Go through it and on to the next gate. Here, follow the direction of the fingerpost diagonally to the right and up to a gate in the drystone wall. The hamlet of Cray is down to the left. In front, the B6160 road goes over Kidstones Pass to Bishopdale. From the gate, follow the path to a gateway just below the rocky hillside. Go through and along the path to another gateway and then up to the right across a pasture. Go through the small gate, with fingerpost, and up to a boggy plateau. Pick your way with care across this, going via a ranging post to a fingerpost up to the left by a wall. Follow the wall up a short, steep climb to the summit with cairn and trig point. If the weather is clear, there are fine views down Wharfedale and across to Langstrothdale.

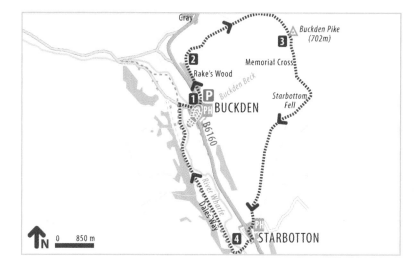

[3] From the summit go over the ladder stile and turn to the right along the wall. From here to Walden Gate, passing the Memorial Cross (to Polish airmen), is about a mile of usually boggy ground. There are peat hags over to the left, and the fluffy seedheads of bog cotton. Go through the small gate in the wall to the right. This is Walden Rd, the old packhorse track. The path descends, becoming a rough track, then a walled lane. On the hill to the left can be seen the remains of a lead smelting chimney. Descend to Starbotton, go left along the B6160 to the end of the village, turn right at the fingerpost and go down the little lane to the footbridge.

[4] Go over, turn right and follow the Dales Way upstream. Sandpipers and grey wagtails are to be seen, and in summer there are bellflowers. The path leaves the river and crosses fields to a plantation whose trees include Norwegian maple, copper beech and Wellingtonia. A few yards past the building, a fingerpost indicates the way back to the riverside. Follow this to an opening in the wall. Go through, turn right over the packhorse bridge and go up the lane to Buckden.

Cotterdale & River Ure

START Appersett,
DL8 3LN, GR SD858907

DISTANCE 7½ miles (12km)

SUMMARY Difficult only
because the track over the
moors can be intermittent;
the rest is straightforward

MAPS OS Explorer OL19 Howgill Fells
& Upper Eden Valley; OS Landranger
98 Wensleydale & Upper Wharfedale

WHERE TO EAT AND DRINK
Nowhere in Appersett, but a
large choice of pubs and cafés
1 mile away in Hawes

Cotterdale is one of the forgotten valleys in the Yorkshire Dales – a dead end for
cars and therefore excellent for walkers.

1 Leave Appersett along the A684 for ¼ mile and just after the
second bridge take the stile on the lane that leads east to Hardraw.
Here the path heads north steeply through a small plantation for
½ mile till it reaches the Pennine Way on the shoulder of the hill.

2 Turn left onto the bridleway and climb for barely ¼ mile before
there is a bridleway leading towards Cotterdale. At an unsignposted
gate, left, enter South Wood and meander downhill along a broad
drive. The path heads clearly into Cotterdale and follows the road end
over the river.

3 Just over the river turn left alongside the river across fields for
½ mile. The footpath then leaves the river, cutting up to the road
out of Cotterdale. Cross the tarmac and take the footpath leading
directly up the slopes opposite. There is a fence on the high shoulder
before the path drops back down to the main road, past two small
plantations. The next ¼ mile is tricky as there is a footpath passing just
to the west of Mossdale Head Farm, but it may be easier just to follow
the farm track past the farmhouse.

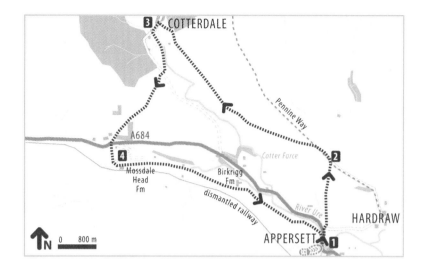

4 Following waymarkers, go left between Mossdale Head Farm buildings and down Mossdale Beck to the embryonic River Ure. Go forward and climb a rusty gate in a hedge ahead. Go along a track in the next field. The track becomes a broad footpath: follow it for 1 mile past Birkrigg Farm and leave it at a triple footpath sign, turning right through valley bottom fields and up a wooded hillside. Turn left and follow stiled pastures for a mile to rejoin the River Ure for a riverside walk to New Bridge. Follow a field path alongside the road to Appersett.

Points of interest

Cotterdale village used to be the centre of a thriving coal-mining community but now is a quiet, dead-end village – attractive but with only twelve houses.

Mossdale waterfalls, above Mossdale Head, was visited during a very wet summer by the artist W.M. Turner, who stayed at nearby Hardraw Falls.

START Jervaulx Abbey, tea rooms
car park, HG4 4PH, GR SE169857

DISTANCE 7½ miles (12km)

SUMMARY Moderate

MAPS OS Explorer OL302
Northallerton & Thirsk; OS Landranger
99 Northallerton & Ripon

WHERE TO EAT AND DRINK Jervaulx
Abbey Gardens café and tea garden,
open April to October (T01677-460391);
The Cover Bridge Inn (T01969-623250)

A low-level walk through pleasant parkland, along quiet country lanes and
delightful riverside paths.

①   From the car park go left along the A6108 for almost ½ mile
and, just past the bridge over Lee Gill Beck, turn right through a gate
waymarked with a yellow arrow. Go along the path ahead and through
another gate and, at the confluence of Lee Gill beck and the River Ure,
turn left, upstream. Stay close to the river, on your right, for 2 miles
(the final part being along the River Cover) to reach Cover Bridge.

②   Turn right over Cover Bridge, hump-backed and built in 1766,
and continue past olde worlde Cover Bridge Inn. Go right at a road
junction and cross the River Ure using Ulshaw Bridge. Beyond, go
right, passing on your left the Catholic church of St Simon and St Jude.
Keep going forward for almost ½ mile and, where the road swings left,
continue straight ahead along an unsurfaced track. The disused water-
driven corn mill you pass on leaving the surfaced road is Danby High
Mill; the one seen from the unsurfaced road, near a tidy cottage, is
Danby Low Mill. Enter Danby Low Park through a gate and continue
through the parkland using a carriageway which soon turns towards
Danby Hall, the splendid Elizabethan home of the Scrope family. Turn
right on approaching the hall gates, passing an ancient oak, and make
for a metal gate ahead, not the wooden one on your right. Continue
eastwards, keeping close to the lower edge of a field, and exit through
a white gate in a fence. Cross four fields to reach isolated St Oswald's

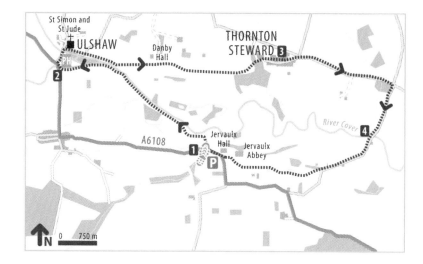

church. This little church, with its medieval bellcote and two bells, is the oldest in Wensleydale.

3   Continue along the road for ½ mile to the village of Thornton Steward from where, because it is set a little above the surrounding countryside, the views of lower Wensleydale are extensive. Leave the village at its eastern end and go along Longdike Lane. After 1 mile, at a crossroads, turn right along Kilgram La for ½ mile to recross the River Ure on a bridge that is said to have been built by the Devil in one night.

4   Continue along Kilgram La for a further ½ mile, passing Kilgram Grange, and where it curves left continue straight ahead to enter Jervaulx Park. The way ahead is clear, the parkland magnificent and soon the walk climaxes when the theocratic remains of Jervaulx Abbey, silent and haunting, meet the eye. The car park is very close now but tarry awhile, for the Abbey merits more than a passing glance.

The Lanes of Long Preston

START The Green at Long
Preston, outside the Maypole
Inn, BD23 4NJ, GR SD835582

DISTANCE 7½ miles (12km)

SUMMARY Easy walking on
mainly good green lanes

MAPS OS Explorer OL2 Yorkshire
Dales: Southern & Western Areas;
OS Landranger 98 Wensleydale
& Upper Wharfedale

WHERE TO EAT AND DRINK
The Maypole (T01729-840219)
and Boars Head (T01729-
840217), both in Long Preston

A quiet walk through a mix of farmland and forestry, with open views over the
Settle limestone scars, the Three Peaks and over to Pendle Hill.

1 From Maypole Green head up the tarmacked lane towards
the school. Pass the school on the right and carry straight on down
Scalehaw La (do not turn right the church). After ½ mile the
tarmac runs out at Hewitt House on the left but the lane itself carries
on down to the river and a small planked bridge.

2 Once you've crossed the river, turn left and sticking close to the
river pass through two fields before arriving at a ladder stile (gate next
to it). Carry on alongside the river, through two more gates, before
crossing a small tributary and bearing right uphill. Pass through a gate
as the green path heads up, initially steeply and then levelling off. An
isolated barn stands to the left – a classic Dales scene. After ¾ mile the
path is joined by a small stream on the right and this bends to the left.

3 Cross the stream and then join a lane (Langber La). Turn left and
follow the lane past embryonic plantations and forestry for 2 miles
until it ends on meeting the quiet Malham–Settle road.

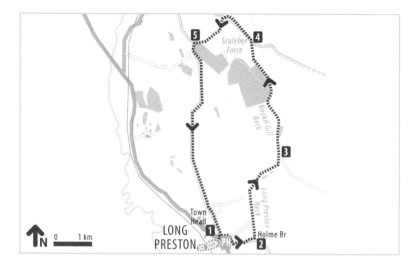

[4] Turn left and almost immediately there is signpost to Scaleber Force, which is an impressive waterfall and worth taking the time to view. Return to the road and follow it for ½ mile. Ignore the signpost to the right for Stockdale Farm but 50yds further, take the left turn into Lambert La (this is part of the Pennine Bridleway).

[5] This green lane wanders and winds its way for a further ½ mile before joining the old road from Settle to Long Preston. Not now suitable for motors, the high-level route passes woodland on the left and then opens up with some wonderful views over Pendle and the Forest of Bowland. After 1½ miles the road becomes firmer and starts to drop towards the village of Long Preston, finishing 50yds from the Maypole Inn and a very welcome pint.

Further information

Scaleber Force has a drop of 20ft and is situated in a beautiful, small copse. It is very easy to view and there are often many people around.

START Horton, main car park – 50yds
from the Three Peaks café (pay &
display), BD24 OHE, GR SD810722

DISTANCE 7½ miles (12km)

SUMMARY The easiest of the
Three Peaks of Yorkshire, but a
tricky scramble to the summit

MAPS OS Explorer OL2;
OS Landranger 98 Wensleydale
& Upper Wharfedale

WHERE TO EAT AND DRINK
The Three Peaks café (T01729-860333)
or the Crown Inn (T01729-860209) are
popular and full of interest and history

Pen y Ghent, at 2,278ft/694m, towers over Horton and offers an interesting
circular walk with fine views from the summit.

① From the car park turn south past the café and towards the
church. Follow the road when it bends left past the church and then
take the left turn just before the river is met. You are in old Horton
here, but after 50yds cross the stream on a small bridge and you will
see Horton primary school ahead. Pass the school and follow the quiet
road to the splendidly named farm of Bracken Bottom. Just before the
farm, turn left through a gate and small stile and then onto the open
fellside. Climb the hillside due east for 1½ miles on an eroded path
(repaired in places) till you arrive at the famous hole in the wall on the
shoulder of Pen y Ghent.

② Pass through the hole and turn left. The 'climb' up Pen y Ghent is
now revealed and involves a minor scramble. There is one point where
hands may be needed but the biggest challenge is the eroded nature
of the climb, thousands of boots making part of the path smooth and
slippery. However, soon you pop out onto the summit ridge with the
large cairn and seating area 200yds away. The route then crosses over
the wall at the summit and heads north-west and then north down the
edge of the steep escarpment.

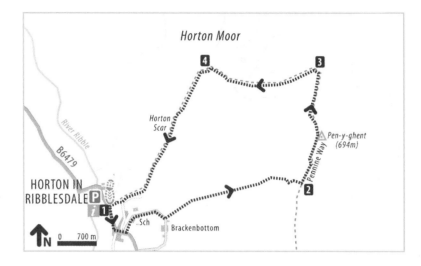

3) At the foot of the escarpment take the newly repaired path left as it heads straight down the hillside – the old Three Peaks path heading straight on. The erosion on the old path was shocking; this fine new path erased one of the main difficulties in completing the Three Peaks.

4) Follow the new path due west till it arrives at a double ladder stile. Cross over and then take the left track signposted back to Horton. The Three Peaks route carries on up the fell opposite. You will be in a walled lane; follow this for 2 miles all the way to Horton village, emerging just opposite the Three Peaks café.

Points of interest

Walkers clock into the Three Peaks café as their start and finish point. The challenge is to complete Pen y Ghent, Ingleborough and Whernside within 12 hours; on a Saturday in summer there is a constant stream of people on the hills.

START Ripley town square,
HG3 3AY, GR SE284605

DISTANCE 7½ miles (12km)

SUMMARY Easy woodland
paths or roads

MAPS OS Explorer 298 Nidderdale;
Landranger 99 Northallerton & Ripon

WHERE TO EAT AND DRINK Castle
Tea Rooms, Ripley (To1423-770152,
open 12–6pm, closed Mon); The
Boars Head, Ripley (To1423-771888)

A walk through a wooded glen and along the Nidderdale Way towards the villages
of South Stainley and Nidd.

1 From the cobbled town square take the road north past the
garage on the left, and the post office on the right, towards the end of
the town. Turn left past the tennis courts to follow a Nidderdale Way
sign. Cross the B6165 road into Birthwaite La and follow it for ½ mile
to a sign for Slate Rigg Farm.

2 At this point fork right along a grass track; a blue arrow on a
yellow background marks the way. Follow the track past a plantation
on the right. After a further 300yds the Nidderdale Way turns right at
a signpost and drops down a path through a wood to a gate. After the
gate turn right down the field and go over an arched bridge to cross the
beck. Go up the field to a gate with arrows. Go through it and veer left
past a small brick building on your left. Follow the contour of the hill,
keeping the pine trees on the left, and go down to a gate in a stone wall.
Follow the path towards marshy ground and, keeping the marsh to the
left, continue for 400yds until a tower with a water pump can be seen.

3 At this point pass into the field with the tower and leave the
Nidderdale Way. From the gate walk up the field to High Cayton
Farm. Go through a mesh gate into the fold yard and out onto the
farm road, which leads to South Stainley. Follow the track down
to the A61, leaving Cayton Ghyll Farm and Cayton Grange on the
right. Cross the A61 and walk down the side of the Red Lion pub

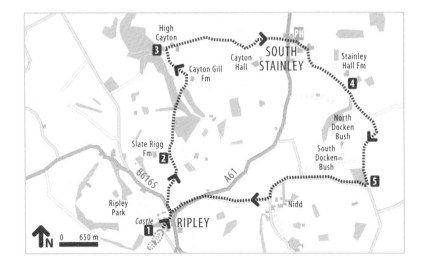

into Stainley village. Go past St Wilfred's church and out to Stainley Hall Farm.

4) Leaving the farm on the left, cross the bridge over Stainley Beck and follow the track for ¾ mile to the junction with Riggs La. Follow the lane to the right down to Prince William Wood (on the left) and Docken Bush Whin (on the right). Shortly after this you will reach the Brearton to Nidd road.

5) Turn right towards Nidd and follow the road into the village. Just before the village, turn right over a disused railway bridge and walk to the junction with the A61. Cross and walk south ½ mile to Ripley and the start of the walk.

Points of interest

Outside Ripley, the castle is All Saints' church, with musket ball marks on the walls said to have been caused by Oliver Cromwell's men. The old stocks stand in the town square.

Thwaite, Muker & Keld

START Thwaite, DL11 6DR,
GR NY892982

DISTANCE 7½ miles (12km)

SUMMARY Moderate walking
along the Pennine Way, but the
riverside section is easy

MAPS OS Explorer OL30 Yorkshire
Dales: Northern & Central Areas;
OS Landranger 92 Barnard
Castle & Richmond, and 98
Wensleydale & Upper Wharfedale

WHERE TO EAT AND DRINK
The Kearton Country Hotel,
Thwaite (T01748-886277); there is
a pub and tea shop in Muker

A simply lovely walk in Upper Swaledale, taking in some walking by the river and
skirting Kisdon Hill.

[1] Take the lane eastwards past the front of the guest house and
follow the Pennine Way behind a farmhouse at the end of the village.
After a few yards pass through a stile into a field. Follow the path,
keeping Muker Beck on the right, and head for two stiles. Go between
a barn and an electricity pole. Go over two more stiles and bear left
over a small bridge. Go over a wall stile and keep the wall on your
right to another stile. Bear right to a large barn, pass in front of it
and head for a stile onto the beck side. Follow the path to a road, and
follow this to Muker. Bear left past the village store, passing the church
and the public hall to the right. Bear right and turn left down a snicket
to a sign, 'Footpath to Gunnerside'. Follow this path over several stiles
to reach the river bank.

[2] Turn right and over a stile and footbridge. Climb steps and turn
left up a steep rise. Turn left uphill and when the path joins a well-
defined track, follow it for about 2 miles to a small footbridge near the
ruined smelt mill, behind which is a waterfall. Go through the gate
and climb up the steep track through another gate. The track now falls
gently to another gate. Walk a few yards and leave the track to join the
Pennine Way. Cross East Gill Force over the bridge, bear right, and
climb a short rise to a handgate. A Pennine Way sign indicates Keld,
which is only a short way right.

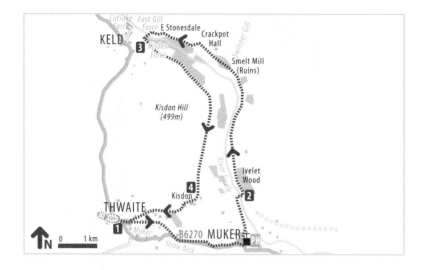

3 Our walk goes to the left. Go through a gate at the end of a wall lane and climb gently between two small hummocks. Bear right past a pile of stones and a Pennine Way sign. Continue ahead through a gap in the wall near a Pennine Way sign. Follow the footpath by the wallside and climb gradually. Care is required on this part of the walk; it is often muddy and rocky. Follow the path, which levels out, following the flank of Kisdon Hill. Go over a stile, then another to reach a gate. After two wall gaps, a gentle climb and a series of stiles, head down towards a derelict house and Pennine Way sign. Turn right and head for a small barn; take the path westwards through a gate and down to Kisdon House.

4 Continue through a second gate and around the back of the house. After a few yards turn left near a Pennine Way sign. After passing a calf house on the right, bear half-right and head for a stile. Continue downhill towards another stile and a Pennine Way sign. Follow the wall to the field bottom and turn right towards a gate and small bridge. Cross the bridge and a field, then go through a gate back to Thwaite.

Whernside from Ribblehead

START Ribblehead,
LA6 3AS, GR SD767794

DISTANCE 7½ miles (12km)

SUMMARY Difficult due to
height and a tricky descent

MAPS OS Explorer OL2;
OS Landranger 98 Wensleydale
& Upper Wharfedale

WHERE TO EAT AND DRINK
In the summer there is often a van
in the parking area serving hot, cold
drinks and burgers; the Station Inn
(T01524-241274) is only 200yds away

The highest mountain in Yorkshire (2,414ft/736m), Whernside offers a challenge
particularly in cloud, but has at least a high start.

1 The path leads towards the viaduct from the roadside parking,
just where the road from Settle meets that passing from Ingleton to
Hawes. After 130yds, and before you reach the viaduct, a path heads
to the right and climbs steeply for a few feet until it draws alongside
the rail tracks. Heading north for 1½ miles, the path sticks closely to
the eastern side of the railway, climbing slightly and passing the now
decrepit Blea Moor station.

2 Turn left over the rail lines and for the next ½ mile climb sharply
north/north-west up the flanks of Whernside. A stile appears on your
left where there is a division of the path.

3 Climb over the stile and head towards the higher parts of the
mountain in a more westerly direction. The path is eroded in places
but much of it has been efficiently repaired, with large boulders
dropped into the peat hags to create the path.

4 After a further mile of steady climbing and increasingly
impressive views, the path joins the main ridge of Whernside and
after a further ½ mile leads to the summit. A wall leads over the
summit and the trig point is just to the west, so climb it and take in

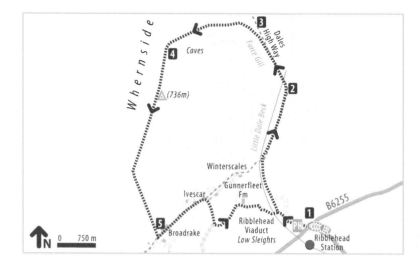

the excellent views north towards the Howgills and the southern Lake District. The path then carries on along the ridge before dropping gently for ¾ mile. Things are about to change, though. The path turns left and drops steeply for 300ft down a severely eroded path. Repairs are being made to the path, so hopefully it will soon be much improved. The descent starts to flatten at the first of two kissing gates.

5 When a cluster of buildings are met, do not follow the main track but turn left onto a bridleway which leads for ½ mile to the farm at Ivescar. Follow the lane right for a few hundred yards, then turn sharp left on the tarmac to Winterscales Farm. Before the farm is the outdoor centre at Gunnerfleet; turn left through a gate with Ribblehead viaduct directly ahead. The viaduct is reached in 5mins; pass under it and join the outbound path back to your car.

Points of interest

Building at Ribblehead started in 1870 and it took four years to complete. It is 440yds long and 104ft high; 1.5 million bricks were used and around 100 'navvies' were killed in its construction.

Askrigg Waterfalls & Worton

START Askrigg, small car park
at the east end of the village,
DL8 3HG, GR SD951912

DISTANCE 8 miles (13km);
shorter version 7 miles (11 km)

SUMMARY Easy walking, but some
steep paths in the waterfalls

MAPS OS Explorer OL30 Yorkshire
Dales: Northern & Central Areas;
OS Landranger 98 Wensleydale
& Upper Wharfedale

WHERE TO EAT AND DRINK There
are several pubs and cafés in Askrigg;
The White Rose (T01969-650515) was
the setting for many of the scenes
from the James Herriot TV series

A walk of real contrasts, with some great views from the scars above Worton and
some spectacular waterfalls and walking in the woods at Whitfield Gill.

[1] Leave Askrigg along Cringley La, opposite the Market Cross,
signposted 'Footpath Aysgarth–Worton Bridge'. Where the lane turns
left, go through a stile on your right and cross a field to the dismantled
Wensleydale Railway. Go left along it briefly and descend some
steps on your right. Take the flagged path across three stiled fields to
Worton Bridge, which crosses over the River Ure, and continue steeply
uphill to Worton.

[2] Turn right along the A684 and almost opposite a bus shelter go
through a gate signposted 'Footpath to Bainbridge'. Go half-right up a
field to a signposted stile below a wooded bank. Climb steeply through
the wood, going westwards along Worton Scar for almost ½ mile,
and on leaving the wood continue westwards across stiled fields with
a wall and a wood on your right. Cross a signposted stile in the wall
on your right, descend stiled fields to the Semer Water road and go
right along it to Bainbridge. Go through the village, northwards, along
the Askrigg road, cross the River Ure using Yore Bridge and continue
along a stiled, paved path across a field on your right.

[3] Turn left between the arches of a railway bridge and cross a
packhorse bridge. Go half-right along a path behind Grange Cottage

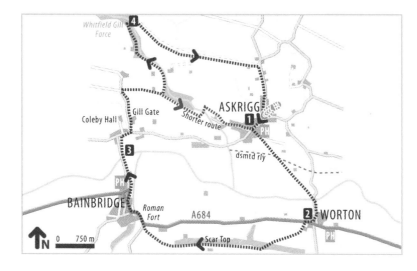

and over two stiles to a road. Turn left in front of Grange Cottage and turn right up a cul-de-sac just before Grange Bridge. Climb steeply past Gill Gate Farm on your right and, where the road turns left, turn right at a stile signposted 'Mill Gill'. Continue eastwards over two stiled fields to a signposted path to Mill Gill Force, a 70ft-high waterfall in a wooded gorge.

4 Retrace your steps to the sign and follow the signs down Mill Gill to Askrigg to complete a shortened version of the walk. Alternatively, follow the numerous yellow markers for a mile-long scramble upstream to Whitfield Gill Force, a 58ft-high waterfall. Now, follow the signpost directions to Low Straits La, bearing right down the gill, to cross a footbridge and climb a steep wooded path. At its top, cross a stile into Low Straits La. Go eastwards along this for a mile and when it reaches the Muker–Askrigg road turn right, downhill, to Askrigg.

Points of interest

Whitfield and Mill waterfalls are two of the most popular and spectacular waterfalls in the Dales.

Askrigg was the setting for Darrowby in James Herriot's *All Creatures Great & Small.* Crinkley House was the surgery.

Gilling West to Ravensworth

START Gilling West, near the Angel Hotel, DL10 5JW, GR NZ182049

DISTANCE 8 miles (13km)

SUMMARY Easy/moderate

MAPS OS Explorer 304 Darlington & Richmond; OS Landranger 92 Barnard Castle & Richmond

WHERE TO EAT AND DRINK
The Shoulder of Mutton, Kirby Hill (To1748-8222772), walkers are made very welcome here

A very pleasant walk linking a number of quiet villages, where time seems to pass comfortably without stress. One steep climb.

[1] Leave the village at the north end of Gilling Bridge, going left at a public footpath sign and through a gap in the wall ahead. Pass Town End Farm and go west through fields on a clear route for 1 mile to Hartforth. Turn left at farm buildings and take a broad track, Jagger La, over Hartforth Beck using an ornate bridge. Go right through a white gate and take a path across a field, with Hartforth Hall and a ruined church visible on your right. Cross a metal footbridge and turn left, upstream, edging a field. At a gap near a rusty gate turn left along a track to the old Hartforth Saw Mill. Follow the yellow markers left, round the mill, and cross a plank bridge to a stile near a gate. Turn right, upstream, through delightful stiled and gated meadows to Comfort La, just south of Whashton Bridge.

[2] Cross (the lane, not the bridge) and continue upstream close to Holm Beck, where herons are often seen on your right. Soon after passing a small brick pump house, and where the beck comes down from the right, go straight ahead across a field along a right of way but with an undefined route, aiming for a stile where the hedge ahead ends. Continue ahead over two stiles, aiming for the top inset right corner of the meadow. Cross a stile near a gate on your right, partly hidden by hawthorn bushes, and go forward to another stile just past some holly and hawthorn bushes. Turn left over a stone stile and go diagonally right over the next two stiled pastures, with good views of ruined Ravensworth Castle ahead, to reach a road.

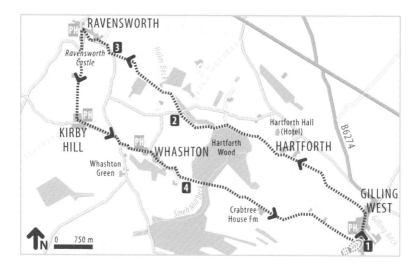

③ Turn right for ½ mile to enter delightful Ravensworth village. Go through it as far as the Bay Horse Inn. Turn left, passing the primary school, and where the road bends right go straight ahead through a handgate near a gate marked 'Larklands'. Continue up a track for a short distance to a stile on your left, tucked in between two ash trees. Go over the stile, then right, diagonally, up rough pasture, heading for a stile where a wall meets a hawthorn hedge. Go up the side of two fields and climb steeply on to Kirby Hill, which is well worth exploring. Leave this little hilltop village along the road past the church on your right and the Shoulder of Mutton on your left. After ½ mile go straight over a crossroads to reach, after another ¼ mile, Whashton village. At the bottom of the village bear right along a lane marked 'No Through Road'. Go downhill for ¼ mile and, immediately after crossing a white railed cattle grid, turn left along a field and out through a gate.

④ Follow the uphill path, between trees, with Hartforth Wood on your left. Cross Smelt Mill Beck on stepping stones and continue eastwards along Leadmill La to Jagger La. Go left along it for a few yards, then right along a clear farm road past Crabtree House Farm into Waters La and so back to Gilling West.

Ramsgill to Lofthouse

START Ramsgill, HG3
5RL, GR SE119709

DISTANCE 8 miles (13km)

SUMMARY Moderate; a pleasant
walk, in part along the Nidderdale Way

MAPS OS Explorer 298
Nidderdale; OS Landranger
99 Northallerton & Ripon

WHERE TO EAT AND DRINK
The Crown Hotel, Lofthouse
(T01423-755206); the Yorke Arms,
Ramsgill (T01423-755243)

A lovely walk in Upper Nidderdale, following the River Nidd, before returning over
the high moors.

1 From Ramsgill take the route out of the village towards
Bouthwaite. In Bouthwaite turn left just past the chapel and follow the
Nidderdale Way sign, going along a lane and left into a farmyard. Go
through the yard and over a wooden bridge which spans Lul Beck.
Over the bridge go right over a stile in the wall. Follow the woodside
up to a set of wooden steps over a high wall. Turn left and follow the
path along the shawl to a second set of steps. In front now is a farm
house: pass to the right of this and onto a chalk stone road. At the next
gate turn slightly uphill towards a plantation. Keep to the left of the
plantation and go over two stiles. At the second stile turn left and go
down to a road.

2 Ignore the Nidderdale Way sign straight across and turn right
along the road towards Lofthouse. After ½ mile take the Nidderdale
Way to the right and cross the fields to Lofthouse village. The path
reaches the road at the side of the Crown Hotel. Turn right up the hill
towards Masham and continue uphill on the road for about 1 mile.

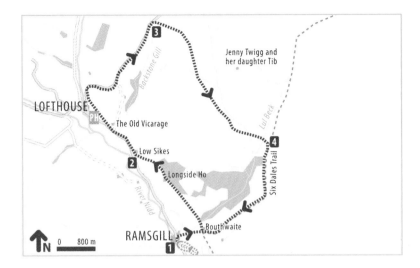

3. Turn right off the road past a sign indicating 'Not Suitable for Vehicles'. Follow the track to a gate with a fire warning sign. Just after the gate the track splits: follow the right fork with a dry stone wall on the right until the track is closed in by walls on both sides. To the left can be seen the millstone grit outcrop of Jenny Twigg and daughter Tib on the skyline. The track now begins to drop away down to a bridge over Lul Beck for the second time. After the bridge the track rises to the junction with the route from Low Ash Head Moor shooting box.

4. Take the track to the right, which runs alongside the big plantation and continue to the junction with the track from Dallow Gill and Dalton Lodge. Turn right past another 'Unsuitable for Motor Vehicles' sign and take the very rough road down to Bouthwaite and onto Ramsgill and the start.

Note – The pull to Lofthouse is very steep and long. In addition, the moorland track is exposed; waterproof clothing is recommended.

WALK

60 | Reeth and Langthwaite

START Reeth, DL11 6SW, GR NZ039993

DISTANCE 8 miles (13km)

SUMMARY Moderate walking on
riverside paths and moorland tracks

MAPS OS Explorer OL30 Yorkshire
Dales: Northern & Central Areas;
OS Landranger 92 Barnard
Castle & Richmond, and 98
Wensleydale & Upper Wharfedale

WHERE TO EAT AND DRINK
There is a choice of pubs and
cafés in Reeth; The Red Lion,
Langthwaite (T01748-884218)

A walk through the inspiration for the filming of *All Creatures Great & Small* –
enjoyable and full of interest.

1 From Reeth take the Langthwaite road for ½ mile to reach a stile
on the right signed to Langthwaite, just beyond a house, 'Sleights
Brow'. The way ahead, over meadows, is well signposted with yellow
blobs and arrows and goes along and above the west bank of Arkle
Beck. In the first ½ mile there are at least nine stiles.

2 When you reach a facing gate leading to a farm track, do not
go downhill to the bridge over the beck. Just cross the track and
follow the markers. After ½ mile, where the path goes alongside
a waymarked wall on your right, the way is particularly muddy.
Continue through a small gate, cross a little beck and go past the
front of West Raw Croft Farm. Go over a farm road and a field, then
through a gate and on through another gateway. Take the faintly
trodden left fork uphill to an easily missed footpath signpost. Turn
right here, continue along the field and exit over a stile. Where Fore
Gill Beck crosses the route there is no bridge, but usually it is possible
to cross dry shod. If too much water is flowing, make a short detour
left until a crossing is possible. Once across this feeder go over a stile,
then cross Arkle Beck on a railed footbridge and continue upstream to
Langthwaite.

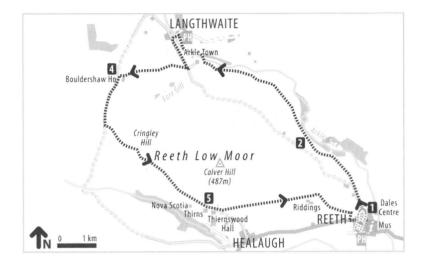

(3) Leave the stream over an ancient bridge across Arkle Beck on your left, then turn left along the road to Arkle Town hamlet. There turn right along a stony track, passing the whitewashed 'White House' on your right, to reach open moor. Follow the track, climbing steeply past Gill House on your left with the way deteriorating and becoming boggy. Head for a wooden gate and continue up trackless moor, passing Bouldershaw House outbuildings. Beyond, go up a farm track to join the quiet Langthwaite–Low Row road.

(4) Turn left for ½ mile to where there are two road signs, 'Z-bend and 1:5'. The way ahead from the hilltop is left through a wooden gate signposted 'Bridleway Only – No Vehicles' and along a track onto Reeth Low Moor. Keep close to the wall on your right and, where the track turns left, bear half-right along a faint track which skirts the side of Cringley Hill. Continue downhill, passing a wire fenced enclosure on your right, then going below a three-walled enclosure on your left.

(5) Where the track forks, go right to a parallel track, which will take you to Nova Scotia and Thirns farms and by Moorcock House back to the moor. Turn right and continue eastwards close to an intake wall on your right and, to the left ahead, the summit of Calver Hill (1,599ft/487m). When Riddings Farm can be seen below on the right, go through a corner gate on your right and along Skelgate La, muddy in places, to join the B6270. Turn left down School Bank into Reeth.

Reeth and Surrender Bridge

START Reeth, DL11 6SW, GR NZ039993

DISTANCE 8 miles (13km)

SUMMARY Moderate walking on moorland, along field paths and country lanes

MAPS OS Explorer OL30 Yorkshire Dales: Northern & Central Areas; OS Landranger 92 Barnard Castle & Richmond, and 98 Wensleydale & Upper Wharfedale

WHERE TO EAT AND DRINK
There are a number of pubs and cafés in Reeth; try the Buck Inn (T01748-884210), which has hand-pulled ales and excellent food

A delightful walk along the moors near Surrender Hill, followed by a riverside walk along the River Swale.

[1] Leave Reeth along the Gunnerside road, B6270, and half-way up School Hill turn right along signposted Skellgate La. At the top go through a gate onto Reeth Low Moor. Turn left by the wall and beyond its corner go westwards over moorland with Riddings Farm below on your left. Join a track from the farm, keeping close to the wall on your left. Cross another stretch of open moor and rejoin a wall on your left. Calver (1,599ft/487m) is on your right here. Continue westwards along an undefined route across moorland, bearing left between spoil heaps to go below a cottage called Moorcock to a farm road.

[2] Go right along past Thirns and Nova Scotia on your left and onto the moor, close to an intake wall. When about 3 miles from Reeth, cross a stile in a facing wall, descend steeply to Cringley Bottom and cross the beck by leaping from rock to rock. Scramble up the steep far bank onto more moorland, where you go half-left along a narrow track; you will come first to Surrender Smelt Mill then to nearby Surrender Bridge.

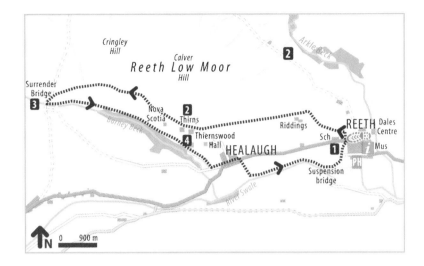

3 Do not cross the bridge (unless for a picnic; there is a nice seating area), but take a left turn and follow the path to the north of Barney Beck. The path sticks above the trees next to the beck, crosses a footbridge over Bleaberry Gill and after 1½ miles reaches the track at Thiernswood Hall.

4 Follow the track down for a further ½ mile to a minor road and turn left into Healaugh. After 300yds past buildings and the Manor House, take the footpath right and head directly down to the river. Join the riverside (often muddy) path and turn left towards Reeth. After ¾ mile you will reach the suspension bridge; do not cross it, but head directly east to join the end of Back La on the outskirts of Reeth.

Points of interest

Surrender Smelt Mill, a scheduled ancient monument, is a reminder of Swaledale's association with lead mining.
   Healaugh village telephone box is quite an attraction, with a carpet, directories and fresh flowers – do leave a donation.

Settle to Malham Tarn

START Settle, public car park just south-west of the market place, BD24 9DW, GR SD819637

DISTANCE 8 miles (13km)

SUMMARY Good tracks and paths, as much of the walk is along the Settle Loop; a steep pull out of Settle and a steep descent at the finish

MAPS OS Explorer OL2 Yorkshire Dales: Southern & Western Areas; OS Landranger 98 Wensleydale & Upper Wharfedale

WHERE TO EAT AND DRINK
The 'Old Naked Man' café, Settle (T07292-32030); the Lion Inn (T01729-822203), a classic Dales pub

A walk that passes over some wonderful limestone scenery along good tracks and with wide-ranging views.

[1] Set off from the far end of the car park, past the toilets, and turn right along a passage-way to the Market. Cross the main road. Facing you is a row of colonnaded shops with cottages above. Go to the left of these, past the Co-op and up steep Constitution Hill. The road turns left at the end of the houses. Look for a stony, walled lane going up to the right, and follow it to a derelict stone barn. At the top, pause for breath and the view. Settle is below you, and the green dome of Giggleswick School chapel is across the valley. If you look down to the left you will see Langcliffe, the Settle–Carlisle railway and the River Ribble. Keep to the track across fields, with the wall to your left, ignoring a path up to the right. A narrow road can be seen coming up from Langcliffe; our path ascends to the lower edge of a wood and continues to join this road at a bend.

[2] Turn right and follow a gated lane up the edge of the wood. Limestone scars are in front of you and there is another fine view back across the valley. Go past a fingerpost to Victoria Cave. Follow the lane over the hill to where it ends abruptly and go forward on a path with the wall on your left. Go through a gateway, beyond which the path is indistinct. Keep in the same direction, with Black Hill on your right, and descend by a wall to the road at Capon Hall.

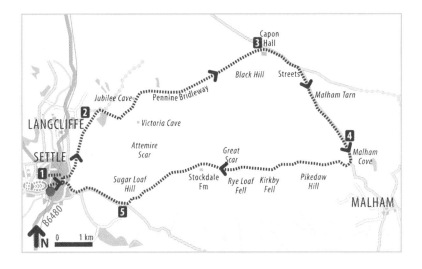

③ Turn right. Where the road forks at a cattle grid, turn right and right again at the next fork. Malham Tarn can be seen to the left, while in the foreground is a ruined smelting chimney. Watch out for traffic on these narrow roads: Malham is a popular area.

④ Go down to Langscar Gate, cross the cattle grid, and turn right on the rough track. Go up to a gateway. Go through and take the path uphill to Nappa Cross, set in a drystone wall. A path comes up from the left through a gate; join this and go to the right, and follow the clear track. Follow it down the side of a steep valley, with Rye Loaf Hill to the left. Beyond Stockdale Farm the walking is easier. This is high limestone country, with scars and canyons – Attermire Scar to the right – and after heavy rain, the underground water jets and bubbles into streams and pools.

⑤ The lane takes you down to a road. Turn right and, taking care as before, follow it to Settle. From the top of the final descent, there is a bird's-eye view of the town.

START Shaw Mills, HG3
3HU, GR SE258625

DISTANCE 8 miles (13km)

SUMMARY Moderate, particularly
if Brimham Rocks is included

MAPS OS Explorer 298
Nidderdale; OS Landranger
99 Northallerton & Ripon

WHERE TO EAT AND DRINK
Information Centre at Brimham
Rocks (T01423-780688); New Inn
at Burnt Yates (T01423-771070)

This is a walk that takes in one of the more attractive sections of the
Nidderdale Way with views along the valley, and also a visit to the extraordinary
Brimham Rocks.

1 From Shaw Mills take the road to Bishop Thornton. At the top of
Thornton Bank turn left into Cut Throat La past a 'No Through Road'
sign. Continue down the walled lane to a small farm on the left and a
stream with a footbridge. The lane is joined from the left by another
track also coming up from Shaw Mills. Continue to follow the walled
track to Hatton House Farm. Just past the farm the track becomes a
chalk stone road.

2 Approximately ⅓ mile further, turn left onto a tarmac road.
Another ⅓ mile brings you to the Nidderdale Way coming in from
the left at Black House. Continue to a cattle grid and, ignoring the
new road to the right, pass over the grid and down into the yard of the
former Woodfield Mill. Pass the mill on your right and go through a
gate to a Nidderdale Way sign pointing to the right across a field to a
gap in a drystone wall on the left. Turn through the gap and follow a
number of arrows down to a stream and a wood on the right. Cross
the stream, and go through a gate up the field with a stone wall on the
right. Go through three more gates, with the wall now on the left, to
a T-junction at the third gate. At this point we turn right, leaving the
Nidderdale Way, and walk the 200yds to Park House Farm.

3 Turn left just before the farm and walk up to a gate into a
meadow. Go through the gate and, keeping the wall on the immediate

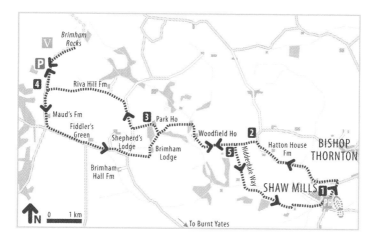

left, climb up the field, go over two stiles and on to a track. Ignore the arrows the other side of the track and turn right along it; we have now regained the Nidderdale Way. Follow the track and Nidderdale Way signs to Brimham Rocks. The last part of the Way is a path across a peat and bracken moor, which can be very boggy in winter.

④ When reaching the road, turn right to visit Brimham Rocks. Return back down the road to this point to continue. Walk about a mile to a crossroads, passing Mauds Farm on the left. Turn left at the crossroads and walk downhill towards Burnt Yates, passing Fiddlers Green and Shepherds Lodge, both on the left. After about 1 mile the road turns sharp right. At this point leave the road and follow a lane straight ahead to Brimham Lodge Farm. Pass through the farm, with the house on the right, down to the point at which we left the Nidderdale Way on the outward leg of the walk. Turn right and follow the original path past Woodfield Mill back to the sign which points to the right and down to Black House.

⑤ Just before Black House turn left through a gate, down to Thornton Beck. Cross the footbridge and turn left to a stile over a drystone wall. Go over the stile and walk up the field to the woodside. Turn left and follow the wood to a track, which in turn changes to a farm road. Ignore the arrows to the right which lead to Burnt Yates and follow the track to Shaw Mills, passing three farms along the way. The track eventually meets Pye La in Shaw Mills. Turn left over Pye La bridge and back to the Nelson Inn.

Simon's Seat

START Cavendish Pavilion,
BD23 6AN, GR SE078552

DISTANCE 8 miles (13km)

SUMMARY Moderate to hard. NB:
dogs are not allowed on the fell as
it is a game-bird breeding area

MAPS OS Explorer OL2 Yorkshire
Dales: Southern & Western Areas;
OS Landranger 104 Leeds & Bradford

WHERE TO EAT AND DRINK
The Cavendish Pavilion (T01756-
710245) has good food, tea and cakes

An often steep but pleasant climb through valley and moorland with excellent
views, before returning along the impressive River Wharfe.

[1] Leave the car park and turn left on the main road into the village.
Note the tithe barn opposite. Go past the post office tearooms and
through the hole in the wall to the grounds of Bolton Priory. Go
down to the River Wharfe, passing the ruins, and up to the Cavendish
Memorial. Follow the lane down and right to the next car park by the
Cavendish Pavilion snack bar. Cross the river by the footbridge and
turn left on the narrow Storiths road. At the top of the first rise in the
road there is a wicket gate in the stone wall on your right. Go through,
pass the cottage and follow the path up to Posforth Gill. The path
ascends steeply by a waterfall to a delightful spot called the Valley of
Desolation.

[2] Cross the stream by the footbridge and follow the path to a fork.
If you wish to see the next waterfall, take the right fork. You will have
to return as there is no access to the fell. The left-hand path goes up
to a gate and stile. Go over and follow the forestry road up and right,
through the plantation to a gate which brings you out onto the moor.
Follow the track across a ford and up past a stone table to cross the
head of the beck. From here follow the cairns to the largest jumble of
millstone grit boulders. This group is called Simon's Seat, perched on
the edge of an escarpment and with a good view up Wharfedale.

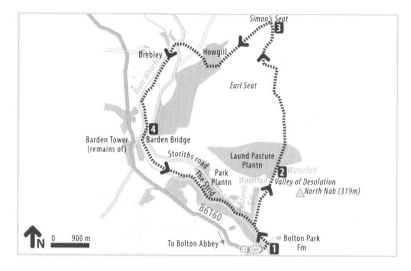

③ Turn left, on a broad track which descends gradually through the heather to a plantation. Turn right down a steep lane to Howgill. Go straight across the narrow road and follow a walled path down to the Storiths road. Cross, then follow the riverside path down to Barden Bridge.

④ Pass the bridge and continue along the river, with Barden Tower on the opposite bank. Soon, the path ascends to woodland. Down to the right, the Strid can be seen – the river is forced into this narrow channel, causing undercurrents and whirlpools. The path goes up to the road and soon you come to the wooden footbridge by the Cavendish Pavilion. Go over and return to the start.

Points of interest

Bolton Priory was founded in 1120 and is beautifully situated. The nave of the priory church is used as a parish church.

Hawes & Green Scar Top

START Yorkshire Dales National Park
Centre, Hawes, DL8 3NT, GR SD876899

DISTANCE 8½ miles (13.5km)

SUMMARY Moderate,
on lanes and paths

MAPS OS Explorer OL30 Yorkshire
Dales: Northern & Central Areas;
OS Landranger 98 Wensleydale
& Upper Wharfedale

WHERE TO EAT AND DRINK
There is a wide range of pubs,
cafés and hotels in Hawes

To the south of Hawes there is some remote moorland steeped in history. The
walking is on good paths or lanes, with some steeper sections. There are great
views over Semer Water and Addlebrough over Wensleydale.

1   Walk into the town centre and look for the footpath, signposted
as the Pennine Way, to Gayle, leaving the main street on the south
side through an arch. The path climbs past the parish church and
continues as a paved 'causey' above Gayle Beck. Note the distinctive
shape of Yorburgh, to your left, as it may well prove useful later. On
reaching the Gayle road, turn left into the village and cross the bridge
before turning left towards Bainbridge.

2   After a few yards only, turn right through a gap stile, signposted
to Marsett. The path is not always distinct on the ground, but heads
directly towards Yorburgh's craggy summit. Go through two gap
stiles to reach a ladder stile. Immediately after crossing it turn right,
heading due south, up the hill. A southerly line is maintained – with
small diversions to ease the gradient on the steepest slopes – until
Blackburn Sike is reached. After following the stream past the shake
holes, turn half-left and cross it, heading south-east. There is no
clear path just here, but aim to cross the skyline about ¼ mile west of
Yorburgh summit.

3   At this point you cross a stile and, turning right, join a
clear bridleway which has come from Burtersett. Follow the way
southwards to the next wall, but after passing through the gate
continue forwards when the track goes right, following a footpath

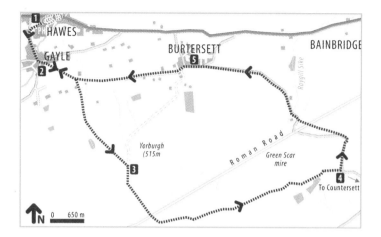

which crosses the Roman road at a pair of gap stiles by a signpost to Marsett. Go forward for 100yds to join the bridleway along Green Scar, turning left along this splendid high-level track, which aims for the prominent scarp of Addlebrough. When Semer Water comes into view, start to descend on a well-made track, crossing the band of limestone to arrive at the road above Countersett.

④ Turn left and follow the road around Hawes End. As it starts to descend, take the footpath across the stile to your right, signposted to Horton Gill Bridge. This crosses the Roman road again. Turn right across the bridge and follow the road down to Burtersett.

⑤ On entering the village, where the road turns right take the turning to the left, going straight ahead at the junction soon after along a walled track signposted to Gayle. When the track ends at a large barn, continue forward past numerous field barns, through a series of gap stiles until, 1 mile from Burtersett, you reach a familiar ladder stile and rejoin the outward route. From this point it is only 1 mile more back to Hawes.

Points of interest

The Roman road linked the fort of Ingleton with that at Brough-by-Bainbridge. Gayle Mill is a fully restored nineteenth-century Victorian saw mill and can be visited as part of the walk.

Addlebrough Circuit

START Askrigg, car park at the east
end of village, DL8 3HG, GR SD951912

DISTANCE 9 miles (14.5km)

SUMMARY Easy walking
(although it can be a little boggy),
generally on lanes or paths

MAPS OS Explorer OL30 Yorkshire
Dales: Northern & Central Areas;
OS Landranger 98 Wensleydale
& Upper Wharfedale

WHERE TO EAT AND DRINK
There is a large choice in
Askrigg and Bainbridge, but
nothing in Thornton Rust

The walk starts in the pretty village of Askrigg, gradually ascending to higher
moors that were popular in our industrial history.

1 On leaving the car park turn left, then left again immediately
over a footbridge. Aim diagonally right up the field, to a stile in the
top right-hand corner. Go over it and continue diagonally across two
more fields, by way of stiles, before dropping onto a track serving
new houses. Turn left for a few yards, then left again at the junction
(footpath signpost to Worton). After 100yds leave the obvious
footpath (which bends left) in favour of that going straight ahead
through the gate. On following it, Worton village becomes visible
ahead, and the path becomes clear as it descends. Go over a number of
stiles to reach a delightful stone-flagged 'causey' leading to the road at
Worton Bridge.

2 Cross the river and fork left at the village centre to reach the
A684. Turn left for 50yds, then take the stile on the right and walk
diagonally left across the field to find the first of eight stiles, which
lead forward in a more or less straight line to finish in woodland. The
path climbs steeply through Worton Scar to emerge on the road. Turn
left and enjoy an easy walk with good views into the dale bottom.

3 Reach Thornton Rust and turn right opposite the village hall.
Keep left on crossing the stream and follow the walled bridleway up
to a plateau, with excellent views back into Wensleydale and forward
to Addlebrough hill. At the lane end, aim for a point just left of

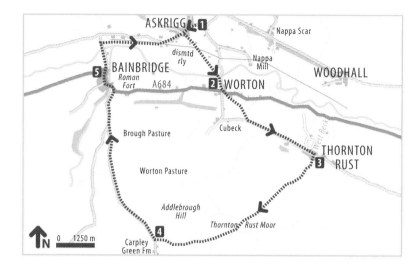

Addlebrough to find the first gate, then continue on the same bearing along a fairly distinct track to pass through a gate in a cross wall, then one in the wall on your right. Go through two more wall gaps while climbing to the southern shoulder of Addlebrough. At least three prehistoric settlement sites, Stony Raise being the most visible, can be seen from this route.

4 Join the lane by Carpley Green Farm and turn right following it down, with views of Semer Water and Green Scar, towards Bainbridge (see Walks 46/47). Avoid the last ¼ mile of road by crossing the stile on the left at the footpath sign, and turning right down the field on a path close to the road. Join the A684 and turn left into the village, using the path across the green, which keeps close to the houses on your right.

5 The path emerges on the road to Askrigg, which you follow to the Ure bridge, leaving it on the far side by a footpath on your right signposted to Askrigg. After one field turn left along the beck, crossing it by an old bridge up-stream, and follow a flagged causey to the road. Turn right, then cross a stile left in 50yds, proceeding diagonally forwards to find a stile in the cross wall. Go over a succession of stiles, taking you directly to Mill Gill. Cross the footbridge and turn right to gain the last of the stone causeys, leading back to Askrigg. Return to the car park by taking the lane opposite the Market Cross, turning left at the end and rejoining the outward route.

START Askrigg, DL8 3HG, GR SD951912

DISTANCE 9 miles (14.5km)

SUMMARY Easy walking along field paths, lanes and some roads

MAPS OS Explorer OL30 Yorkshire Dales: Northern & Central Areas; OS

Landranger 98 Wensleydale & Upper Wharfedale

WHERE TO EAT AND DRINK
The Wheatsheaf, Carperby (T01969-663216) is a good option; or there is a good choice of inns and cafés in Askrigg

A superb scenic walk that shows Herriot Country to advantage – two delightful villages on the north side of Wensleydale and returning via the higher lands.

1 Leave Askrigg along Cringley La, opposite the Market Cross, on a footpath signposted 'Aysgarth–Worton Bridge'. Where the lane turns left go sharp right over a narrow stile beside a gate. Cross a field to the dismantled Wensleydale Railway and go left along it for a short distance. Go through a rusty kissing gate and follow a flagged path diagonally south-east across stiled fields to the River Ure at Worton Bridge.

2 Do not cross the bridge. Instead, turn left along the road and where it bends cross a signposted stile, right, and take the riverside track to Nappa Mill. Continue along the farm road to a triple footpath sign near a stone bridge at the end of Thwaite Holme La. Cross a stile and turn right along a field to a corner stile to the disused railway. Cross and go over a metal ladder stile. Turn right, parallel to the old track. Some 200yds past a railway bridge, just beyond a footpath sign, cross a stile, right, and continue eastwards along the railway track to a kissing gate on your left. Continue half-right over stiled fields to West End Farm. Go along Low La through Woodhall to the Askrigg–Carperby road at the far end of the hamlet. Turn right for ½ mile and, at a 'Parking Place' sign, cross Eller Beck on stepping stones and go over a stile signposted to Carperby.

3 Bear right and take the path through a hazel wood, continuing eastwards along it over a series of stiles to Carperby football field. Turn left, then right, leaving through a gate near a notice 'Private – No Footpath

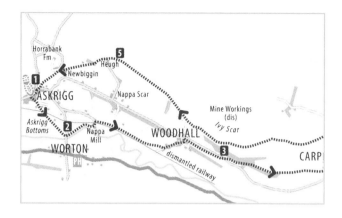

Beyond This Point' and turn right down a track to the road. Go through Carperby as far as the village hall and turn left up Hargill La.

④   Where it divides go left through a red metal gate and along a broad bridleway, westwards, to Carperby Stone Mine where stone flags were quarried. Continue westerly on a green track through a red gate to join the Ox Close Rd. Continue past Wet Groves lead mine below Ivy Scar to reach a gate. Beyond, ford Eller Beck and turn left along a track which goes left through a gate. After a few yards turn left up a steep, stony track and go through a gate at the top. Keep climbing steadily along a clear high-level route, following markers and signposts for more than 1 mile, to reach an isolated house, The Heugh.

⑤   Turn right, briefly, here along walled Heugh La to a wall stile on your left. Cross and go diagonally down two stiled fields into a small wood. At the bottom of this, cross stiled pastures to Newbiggin hamlet. Now go down a walled lane beside a barn marked 'Horrabank' and at the second stone barn go left over a narrow stile near a gate and continue south-west across stiled fields, following markers, downhill into Askrigg.

Points of interest

Carperby has a rather splendid seventeenth-century Market Cross at its western end. The local pub, the Wheatsheaf, is where James Herriot and his wife, Helen, spent their honeymoon in 1941.

68 Dent & Occupation Road

START Dent, car park at west end of village, LA10 5QJ, GR SD704871

DISTANCE 9 miles (14.5km)

SUMMARY A moderate walk, initially very steep, with glorious views

MAPS OS Explorer OL2 Yorkshire Dales: Southern & Western Areas; OS Landranger 98 Wensleydale & Upper Wharfedale

WHERE TO EAT AND DRINK George & Dragon (T01539-625256) or the Stone Close Tea Rooms (T01539-625231), both in Dent.

A tough walk that can be rather boggy (wear a good pair of boots) along Occupation Road, with great views over Dentdale, Deepdale and Whernside

①   From Dent car park cross the road, turn left for a few yards and take the first road on the right. This turns into a stony track, which climbs steeply alongside Flinter Gill onto Little Combe Hill.

②   When you reach a walled track, turn left. This is the Occupation Road, an ancient drovers' route, given its unusual name when the land was enclosed or 'occupied'. After 1¼ miles turn right where the road divides. Nun House Outrake, to the left, is a useful escape route back to Dent if you find the going is too boggy. The hill on your left, on the other side of Deepdale, is Whernside. After a further 1¾ miles the route becomes obscure and particularly boggy. As the track runs out, look half-left and you will see the walls of the track resume.

③   On reaching a road, turn left and then take the first path on your right, signposted 'Mire Garth'. The path veers left crossing a spring, and is marked by white-topped posts. At a farm, cross a concrete path and go through the wooden gate straight ahead. Turn right through a gate alongside kennels and go through a third gate a few yards further on. Turn left and, ignoring the path to the right, continue ahead. The path crosses a spring and runs alongside Deepdale Beck for 50yds before going off to the right. It is now marked by a series of yellow

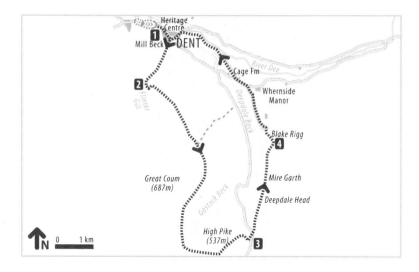

waymarks, stiles and rough footbridges across the springs flowing from Whernside.

4   When, after approximately 1 mile, you reach a metalled track, Dyke Hall La, turn left through a gate and left again at the main road. Immediately after the road crosses the river take the path on your right, signposted 'Church Bridge'. You are now on the Dales Way, which runs along first Deepdale Beck and then the River Dee. At Church Bridge the path veers left onto the main road. Continue left along the road, past the Adam Sedgwick Memorial and back to the car park.

Points of interest

With its winding cobbled streets, Dent is well worth exploring. Although part of the Yorkshire Dales National Park, it is in fact in Cumbria. In the 17th and 18th centuries it was famous for its knitting industry, and spinning galleries can be seen on several of the houses. Dent is also famous as the birthplace of the geologist Adam Sedgwick.

START National Park Centre car park,
Clapham, LA2 5HH, GR SD745692

DISTANCE 9 miles (14.5km)

SUMMARY Long, strenuous walk

MAPS OS Explorer OL2 Yorkshire
Dales: Southern & Western Areas;
OS Landranger 98 Wensleydale
& Upper Wharfedale

WHERE TO EAT AND DRINK
The New Inn in Clapham
(T015242-51203) is an old coaching inn
with a good range of beer and food

A long and strenuous walk but the best route up Ingleborough, passing Gaping
Hill and Ingleborough Cave on the way.

① From the car park cross the river and turn right. As the road
turns left carry straight on, signposted Ingleborough Cave, where
there is a voluntary walk contribution box. After a few initial zigzags,
the wide path sticks to the lakeside and then gradually climbs through
woods for 1½ miles before reaching Ingleborough Cave.

② Carry on past the cave entrance, leaving the trippers behind
before turning sharply left and into the imposing Trow Gill. The path
climbs through the gill and emerges onto the open hillside. After
200yds there is a stile and small gate to the left. Pass through this and
Ingleborough is clearly revealed ahead. To the left there is an excellent
example of limestone pavement – a good place for a stop. The path can
be seen winding up just west of north towards the higher lands.

③ On the right, Gaping Gill is revealed and a small detour can
be made along a path. From the stile to the southern ridge of
Ingleborough is 1½ miles of steady climbing. You will reach a cairn on
the southern tip of the Inglebrough ridge, then head due north along
an initially flat path that soon starts climbing towards the summit
plateau. The path literally pops out onto the large rocky plateau; turn
due west and follow this bearing for 200yds to the summit cairn and

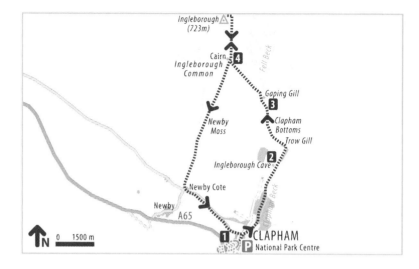

large cross shelter. This can be a confusing place in cloud. From here, retrace your steps all the way to the cairn at the southern tip of the summit ridge.

4   From the cairn, take the less obvious public footpath which heads west of south across the grassy hillside. This path can be intermittent in places but carries on in the same direction for 2 miles until the quiet back road to Clapham from Ingleton is met at the farm of Newby Cote. Turn left and follow the quiet road for 1 mile back into the village of Clapham.

Points of interest

Clapham is a delightful village, with a pretty wooded beck running through it. The naturalist Reginald Farrar lived here, as did, reputedly, the 'Witch of Clapham'.

Gaping Gill is a 1,000ft/305m hole in the limestone bedrock in which water falls, re-appearing again near Ingleborough Cave.

Ingleborough is the second highest hill in Yorkshire (after Whernside). One of the Three Peaks, it casts a very distinctive outline from all directions.

70 Kirkby Malzeard

START Kirkby Malzeard,
HG4 3RS, GR SE234743

DISTANCE 9 miles (14.5km)

SUMMARY Easy

MAPS OS Explorer OL298
Nidderdale; OS Landranger
99 Northallerton & Ripon

WHERE TO EAT AND DRINK
The Queens Head
(T01765-658497) in Kirkby Malzeard

Wide-ranging views are the surprising highlight of this easy walk through quiet countryside.

① Take the Laverton road at the west end of the village street and turn left immediately into the 'back lane'. Follow this as far as the sports field, turning half-right across the field so as to leave it short of the tennis courts. At the cemetery signpost turn right over the stile, instead of going straight ahead, and follow the right-hand hedge to another stile. Cross and continue ahead until, at a gate on the right, you turn half-left to emerge by way of a third stile onto a lane. Turn right and follow the lane to a T-road. Go right again through Laverton village.

② At its western extremity, where the road turns right, go straight ahead along a bridleway. Follow the bridleway, making a sharp turn right at Low Intake Farm, for nearly a mile to a fork. Turn right to Kirkby Moor. Turn left along the road, then right almost immediately (before a farm that is not as shown on the OS map), following the right-hand hedge until Paley's Plantation is reached. The footpath through it soon becomes a clear track leading to a road. Turn left, then right after 200yds, along a bridleway serving the two Biggin farms. After 250yds turn left, leaving Biggin Grange to your right, and continue into Middle Biggin farmyard. Turn left here, through a gate, and go forward up the field to the crest of the hill. After passing through the first gate on the hilltop you are faced by two more in the cross-wall. Pass through the right-hand one and turn half-right, across the field, to a gate visible in the far corner. On leaving it, head for the

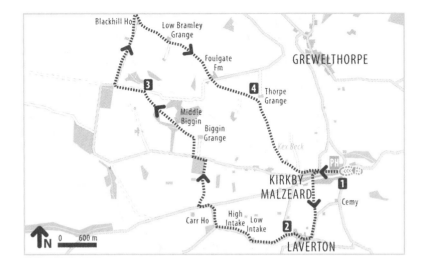

distant barn, the former site of Upper Biggin Farm. Take the gate next to the ruin, then turn half-right to reach a gate leading into Wreaks La.

③ Turn left along this lane for ¼ mile, then right after it becomes a tarred road. Follow this turn north for 1 mile to a right turning just after Black Hill House. Pass Bramley Grange to reach Foulgate Nook, where you cross the stile opposite the house and turn half-left across the field to a stile in the left-hand wall. On crossing it, follow the northern hedge of a narrow field to find the next stile. Go over it and follow the right-hand hedge to a barn, which you go round on the north side. Cross the stile ahead and continue with the hedge on your right towards Thorpe Grange.

④ Turn right at the copse before the farm, pass through a gate on your left, then turn half-right, crossing the field to another gate. Go right through a further gate in quick succession and straight down the field to another. After this, follow the left-hand hedge to emerge on a bridleway by a stream. Turn left and cross the footbridge to reach a hedged green lane. About 150yds after passing a building on the left, turn right over a hidden stile towards a bungalow, but turn left before it, going over two stiles. Pass between wooden sheds, then turn right into a hedge corner, where steps lead down into the lane at the west end of the village.

Embsay Moor

START Embsay car park (near the Cavendish Arms), BD23 6QT, SE009538

DISTANCE 10 miles (16km); short route 3½ miles (5.5km)

SUMMARY Hard, with areas of exposed moorland; possible navigational difficulties if misty

MAPS OS Explorer OL2 Yorkshire Dales: Southern & Western Areas; OS Landranger 103 Blackburn & Burnley, and 104 Leeds & Bradford

WHERE TO EAT AND DRINK The Elm Tree (T01756-790717) and Cavendish Arms (T01756-793980), both in Embsay

This is a long, hard day over some rough moorland that can become wet. However, the rewards make it worthwhile. The shorter version offers a gradual climb up a heather-topped hill to Embsay Crag, a scramble over the rocks, and a steep descent to the reservoir.

1 Leave the rear of the car park, going over a stile and diagonally right to reach a road to the south of the church via some stone stiles and a gate. Turn left along the road, pass the church and, 70yds after the road turns sharp right, go left along a path signed 'Embsay Crag and Reservoir'.

2 Take this path past the farm and over a stile onto a track. Follow the track, which passes through two gates, to open moorland. Note: these gates are across the track, not the ones to the right. For the short route, see below.

3 Now bear right, following yellow waymarkers northwards, along a moorland path with distant Deer Gallows Ridge to the left. After about 1½ miles a more distinct track crosses your line of walk at a signpost.

4 Turn left along it, going towards Rylstone, with good views of Simons' Seat in Wharfedale and Lancashire's Pendle Hill. Continue along this broad track for about 1 mile, to reach some blue waymarkers on the right. Follow these to reach a gate at the end of the moor. Go through the gate and go slightly right, following more blue markers, to join another good track.

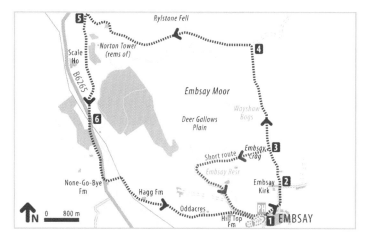

⑤ Follow this downhill, going past a small plantation and then through a gate into a lane. The remains of Norton's Tower are on the hillside to your left. Go straight ahead with a wall, first on your left then on your right, to reach a green lane. Go along this to reach the main Skipton–Grassington road.

⑥ Turn left along it for ¾ mile, as far as None-Go-Bye Farm. Here, go left along a footpath marked 'Embsay'. Keep straight ahead to reach a footpath sign on your right. There, take the path across an old railway line, going past Haggs Farm, then Clark House and Oddacres Farm, to enter the farmyard of Hill Top Farm over a stile. The way ahead is in front of two farmhouses, through a gate and down a slope to cross a dam bank. On joining the road ahead, turn right to go back into Embsay.

Short route: A few yards after the second gate ❷ the path forks half-left to the top of the hill and Embsay Crag. Once you have scrambled down the rocks of the crag, take the path which leads to the right-hand side of the reservoir. At the gate, turn left and follow this quiet, walled road towards Embsay. After 1 mile, when you see some ponds on your right, follow the path on your left, which will take you back to the car park.

Points of interest

The Rylstone area was used in the 1990s film, *The Calendar Girls.*

START Middleham market
place, DL8 4NP, GR SE127877

DISTANCE 10 miles (16km)

SUMMARY Moderate,
only due to length

MAPS OS Explorer OL30 Yorkshire
Dales: Northern & Central Areas; OS
Landranger 99 Northallerton & Ripon

WHERE TO EAT AND DRINK
In Middleham, the appropriately
named Richard III (T01969-623240)
or Black Swan (T01969-622221)

A gentle walk with few climbs but many villages, through spacious, open country.

[1] Go through the archway next to the Richard III hotel and at the
top of the yard turn right, then left just before the castle. The track
skirts the moat and continues to a gate where you go straight ahead,
with the wall on your right, to the next gate. Here, change sides and
proceed with the wall on your left, turning right after 500yds (there is
no clear path) to head for a distant barn. Turn left here, through the
gate, and aim to cross the line of trees on your right about half-way
along their length. Continue forward to join a track dropping through
woodland to Hullo Bridge.

[2] After crossing the River Cover continue to follow the track up
the hill and through two gates to join the lane below Braithwaite
Hall. Turn right along the lane for ¼ mile, then fork left along the
footpath signposted to Caldbergh. Climb slightly to pass above a
small plantation, then follow the indistinct path forwards (keeping the
barn visible ahead on your right hand) to pass through three gates in
succession. Follow the track as it descends gently to Caldbergh. Turn
left here at the footpath sign to East Scrafton and pass between the
house and the farm buildings to reach a gate. Go slightly right to find
steps leading down to a footbridge. After crossing, keep straight ahead
to cross the awkward wooden fence ahead; it is easier further right.
Once in the field, keep the wall on your right to find a footbridge over
a second stream. Continue, still following the wall, to East Scrafton
Hall where you pass through a gate, right, then turn left to another.
Go through to a lane. Turn right and cross the Coverham road, taking

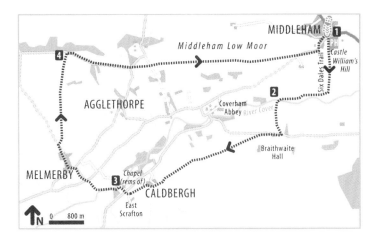

the path signposted to Melmerby. The path descends by steps to a well-hidden, ruined chapel and continues along the river bank to a footbridge.

③ After crossing, climb through woodland and proceed westwards along its upper edge to a stile. Cross and turn right to join a green lane. Arriving on the Carlton road, turn left, then right at the sign for Melmerby. Turn left at the T-road, then right again to head north up the village street of Melmerby. After crossing the cattle grid turn half-right across the moor, as indicated by the footpath sign. The path is faint, but its line is indicated by posts, which lead to a stile. Go over and head for a gate in the north corner of the field. On passing through, continue north across a low ridge to find a stile in the far right-hand corner of the field. Go over two more stiles in quick succession, then cross the gallops to emerge on Common La.

④ Turn right for ¾ mile to a T-road, then leave the road and go straight ahead on a signed bridleway for 2 miles of open walking, with good views on both sides, to reach the road near Middleham. Turn left and follow the road back to the start.

Points of interest

Middleham castle was the residence and in many ways power base of Yorkist king Richard III.

Moors over Keld

Start Keld, DL11 6LL, GR NY892011

Distance 10 miles (16km)

Summary Difficult and exposed walking on high moorland paths; do not attempt in bad or winter weather

Maps OS Explorer OL30 Yorkshire Dales: Northern & Central Areas; OS Landranger 92 Barnard Castle & Richmond

Where to eat and drink The Keld Lodge (To1748-886259) offers food at lunch and in the evening and is open all day.

A superb but strenuous traverse of moorland peat bogs and paths, with glorious views.

1 Leave Keld along a footpath signposted 'Public Footpath to Muker' at the bottom right-hand corner of the hamlet and go along the lane for 400yds to a Pennine Way sign, which directs you left down to the Swale. Cross the footbridge and go straight ahead, close to East Gill Force on your right. This is the first of several waterfalls on this walk. Above the waterfall turn left along a farm track and climb up to East Stonesdale Farm. Continue along an enclosed lane on to Black Moor and keep in the same direction through gated fell pastures. The way is northward passing, on your right, Low Frith and High Frith Farms, and crossing Stonesdale Moor along a stony track. Where it ends, follow a green track to Lad Gill ford.

2 Turn right, climbing Lad Gill Hill along a peaty path, passing fenced pitshafts to reach Tan Hill Inn. Here go left briefly, and left again along the Keld road for 250yds to a sign, right, indicating 'Raven Seat 3 miles'.

3 Turn left here (south-west) along a faint path, an old jagger or coal road parallel to Tan Gill, on your left. Where two sikes meet, cross the gill and continue southwards along the left bank of Stonesdale Beck, past a sheep fold, right. Just beyond where Thomas Gill enters Stonesdale Beck, cross the latter on a plank bridge and climb the south side of Thomas Gill, passing another sheepfold on your left. At the top

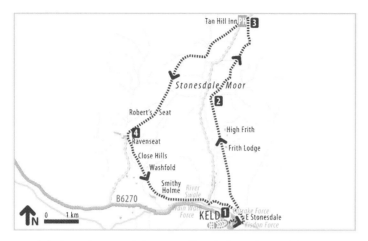

turn left along the rim of Thomas Gill and where the track becomes faint aim for a boundary fence on higher ground and continue along it to where it turns left. Cross a corner stile with large stones on each side of it. Immediately turn left, keeping close to the fence to avoid peat bogs, and when it dips go half-right to ruinous Robert's Seat House. Continue south-west, aiming for a TV mast and descend to a waymarked stile. Cross and follow waymarked posts. Cross Hoods Bottom Beck at Jenny Whalley Force to enter the two-farm hamlet of Ravenseat.

④ Go south-east, roughly parallel to the beck on your right, following yellow markers, past cascading waterfalls and through gated pastures, skirting dramatic Howe Edge and Oven Mouth Gorge. Beyond the Gorge take the lower of two paths past Vast Eddy sheepfold, left. Pass behind empty Smithy Holme Farm to reach a second farm. Beyond this, go left through a gap in a wall and eastward, crossing above Cotterby Scar, with Wain Wath Force in the Swale below. At a facing road turn left, uphill, briefly and go right along a farm road. Pass Carrake Force, below on your right, to reach East Stonesdale Farm, from where you return to Keld.

Points of interest

Tan Hill Inn is England's highest, at 1,732ft/528m, and is famous for its sheep farms.

Moors over the Upper Nidd

START Lofthouse car park, HG3 5SA, GR SE102736

DISTANCE 10 miles (16 km)

SUMMARY Long, mainly easy walking, but two steep climbs

MAPS OS Sheets Explorer 298; OS Landranger 98 Wensleydale & Upper Wharfedale, and 99 Northallerton & Ripon

WHERE TO EAT AND DRINK
The Crown Hotel (To1423-755206), Lofthouse; the Crown Hotel (To1423-755204), Middlesmoor

A real sense of walking in remote countryside – an exhilarating day's walking.

1 From the car park walk up the main street and leave the village by the Masham road, bearing left after a few hundred yards onto a signposted bridleway. This green lane linked the former Fountains Abbey granges, but after 1 mile, at Thrope Farm, you leave it by the gate below the barn, on the right, and climb steeply up the field to the gate visible at the top. Go through and turn left along the fence to another gate. After this you take the steep right turn up the hillside by the fence.

2 By Thrope Plantation the path bends sharply left, continuing to climb to the moor-wall gate. The best of the views appear on passing through the gate and climbing a rocky slope straight ahead, to Ramsden's shooting box.

3 Turn left along a wide track and enjoy splendid views of upper Nidderdale, dominated by Great and Little Whernside, which unfold along the next 4 miles of high-level walking, known as Dale Edge. The track finishes at a long-disused coal mine, whose deep shaft, though fenced, is best avoided.

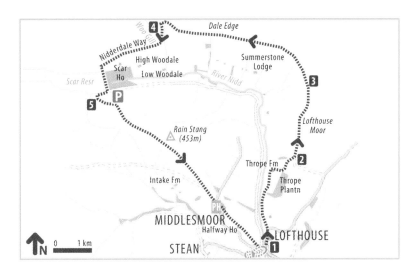

[4] From here, head south down an obvious path, to join a bulldozed track taking you steeply down to cross Woo Gill ford. Climbing again, on the far side, double back to the right at the wall up a stony track, reaching Firth Plantation on your left after a short distance. Go through the gate and continue straight ahead for ¾ mile until you reach another track just above Scar House Reservoir. Turn left and follow it down to cross the dam.

[5] After crossing it, turn right for 300yds, then left up a steep stony track towards Middlesmoor. At the top of the hill, pass through a gate into a walled lane. Follow it down to Middlesmoor, an attractive huddle of stone houses with a pub and shop. Along the right-hand side of the churchyard is a flagged path leading to a wicket gate. Beyond the gate the path descends to a stone stile, then by way of a gate into the farmyard of Halfway House. Continue straight on through a gate and along the right-hand hedge to a stile in the lower right-hand corner of the field. After crossing it, keep the wall on your right to find the next stile, near a barn. Cross the stile and follow the left-hand wall to emerge onto the road at a wide bend. Turn left immediately along the signposted path to Lofthouse, crossing a former railway line, now a road, to reach a footbridge over the limestone gorge of the (frequently dry) Nidd. Turn right after the bridge and after 100yds emerge in Lofthouse.

Semer Water & Addlebrough

START Bainbridge, DL8
3EE, GR SD935904

DISTANCE 10m (16km)

SUMMARY Moderate; mix of
walled lanes and field paths

MAPS OS Explorer OL30 Yorkshire
Dales: Northern & Central Areas;
OS Landranger 98 Wensleydale
& Upper Wharfedale

WHERE TO EAT AND DRINK
The Corn Mill Tea Room, Bainbridge
(T01969-650212) has excellent
sandwiches; Rose & Crown Hotel,
also in Bainbridge (T01969-650735)

A delightful walk taking in a rare site in the Yorkshire Dales – natural water –
and a return over the higher lanes with great views over Wensleydale.

1 From Bainbridge take the A684 Aysgarth road over the River
Bain and turn right before the Stalling Busk road over a stile
signposted 'Semer Water 2 miles'. Bear left along an uphill footpath,
close to a wall on your left, which dips slightly near a walled enclosure
before climbing to the top of Bracken Hill. At the top, Semer Water
comes into view and there are lovely views of Askrigg behind and into
Raydale. Ahead are two stiles. Take the signposted one on the right
and follow the waymarked path through stiled fields to a high ladder
stile near a gate. Go over and immediately turn right, still following
waymarkers, to the River Bain. Follow the stiled path upstream to
Semer Water Bridge.

2 Cross the road and go on to the foreshore of Semer Water, where
lies the Carlow Stone, a large limestone boulder deposited there by
an ice-age glacier. Turn left along the road for ½ mile to Low Blean
Farm and turn right opposite, over a ladder stile signposted 'Stalling
Busk 1 mile'. Just beyond a barn on your left, a stiled path leads close
to the lake but with no access to it. Leaving the lake behind, cross two
stiles into Semer Water Nature Reserve, where steady climbing across
a rough pasture on a good path reaches Stalling Busk's ruined church.

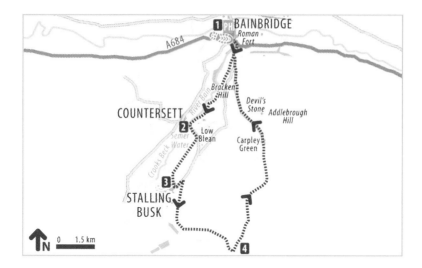

To continue, turn right and immediately go half-left through a ruined wall where a signpost directs you up a 200ft steep climb to ½-mile distant Stalling Busk.

③ Now turn right, then left, to reach the Church of St Matthew, built to replace the ruined one you have just passed. Turn left by Bells Cottage, climb half-way up Butts La and turn right along Bob La. When High La is reached, turn right along it. Continue along this lovely green lane, from which there are some extensive views across Wensleydale and beyond.

④ After 2 miles turn left along Busk La for 4 most pleasant miles to return to Bainbridge, passing, at the mid-way point, Carpley Green Farm from where it is all downhill.

Castle Bolton, Aysgarth Falls & the River Ure

START Castle Bolton car park,
DL8 4ET, GR SE033919

DISTANCE 11 miles (17.5km)

SUMMARY Moderate;
long but easy walking

MAPS OS Explorer OL30
Yorkshire Dales: Northern &
Central Areas; OS Landranger
99 Northallerton & Ripon

WHERE TO EAT AND DRINK There
are tea rooms at the Castle (T01969-
623981); the Bolton Arms at Redmire
(T01969-624336) is very good

Visiting many of the most iconic sites in the Dales, this walk along Wensleydale
is a must for every visitor.

1 From the car park go right over a stile signposted 'Aysgarth
3 miles' and then westwards along an unsurfaced track through fields.

2 After 1½ miles ford West Gill and go left through a gate signposted
'Carperby'. Continue along a path across a rough pasture and through
another signposted gateway. Continue downhill and at the triple
signpost go left for ½ mile into Carperby. Turn right into the village and
opposite the Wheatsheaf Inn go through a gate, then left, southwards,
to Low La. Cross to a stile, beyond which you follow a clear path
through stiled fields into Freeholders Wood. Now bear right, downhill,
to the Carperby road. Turn left and go under a railway bridge, then past
Aysgarth car park and Information Centre on your right to reach the
River Ure. Before crossing it, leave the road and detour upstream for a
close inspection of the Upper Falls, clearly seen ahead.

3 Back at the road, cross Yore Bridge and climb the steps ahead
beside the museum to St Andrew's Church, which is well worth a
visit. Go in front of it and eastwards through the churchyard to cross
a stile into a field. Cross the field to another stile. Cross and continue
with the river close to you on your left, passing the Middle Falls
then the Lower Falls. Keep in the same direction along a clear path
to the entrance to Hestholme Farm on the A684. Go left, crossing

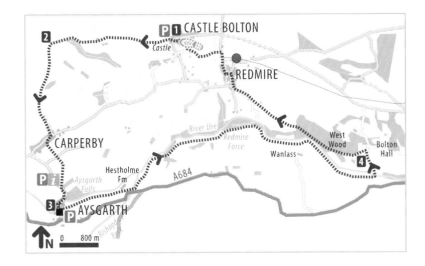

Bishopdale Beck on Hestholme Farm Bridge. Take the first stile on your left and follow the path eastwards, beside the river. At Wellclose Plantation climb the steep path away from the riverside and, at the top of the hill, cross a signposted stile. Turn left and follow yellow marker posts to the top of the field. Turn right along an elevated, stiled path. Continue eastward over four more fields to enter Comlands Wood over a ladder stile and descend a stepped path to Redmire Force. Follow the signs out of the wood, then go left along a field and over another ladder stile. Continue eastwards over fields, following an intermittent track. When High Wanless Farm is seen on your right, join a gated riverside path to a stream with a triple signpost, where you go eastward across some stiled fields to a tree-lined lane. Go left, down the lane, and cross the River Ure on Ford's Bridge.

4 Now take the drive through Bolton Hall Park and, as you approach the Hall, go through a gate, then left, along a track edging West Wood for a mile and out through a kissing gate. Now cross a series of stiled pastures for 1 mile to reach Redmire along Well La. Go right, up the village, and opposite Hogra Farm go left by the village hall. Pass the Bolton Arms and beyond the school go under the railway bridge, then left at the footpath sign, and follow a path parallel to the line serving Redmine Quarry. Where the railway ends, continue across stiled pastures to enter Castle Bolton.

WALK

78 Hawes & the High Moors

START National Park Centre car park,
Hawes, DL8 3NT, GR SD875900

DISTANCE 13 miles (21km)

SUMMARY Hard; remote and long

MAPS OS Explorer OL30 Yorkshire
Dales: Northern & Central Areas;
OS Landranger 98 Wensleydale
& Upper Wharfedale

WHERE TO EAT AND DRINK
The café at Wensleydale Creamery
(T01969-667664); lots of hotels,
pubs and cafés in Hawes

A strenuous walk, in the steps of the drover; there's one demanding climb.

[1] Leave the car park and walk through Hawes on Gayle La to a
stile signposted 'Mossy Lane' opposite Wensleydale Creameries and
take the path across five stiled fields to Mossy La. Continue westwards
across two more fields to the B6255 and go left along it for about
150yds. Where it bends right, go left along an old drove road called
West Cam Rd. It is a tough, uphill slog but you will be rewarded with
magnificent all-round views. At the top, where you cross a ladder stile
beside a gate, have a breather and enjoy what's on offer. The going is
easier now, south-west along an open fell track over Backsides, until,
just past Snaizeholme Plantation, on your right, the stone track climbs
steeply, giving you some fine views of Ingleborough. The Pennine
Way joins West Cam Rd 2 miles from the B6255, meeting it obliquely
from the left. A cairn displaying the words 'Cam Road–Pennine Way
Hawes' in white acknowledges this marriage of routes. The way ahead
continues along a high-level green lane for a further 2½ miles along
the side of Dodd Fell to the junction of West Cam Rd and Cam High
Rd.

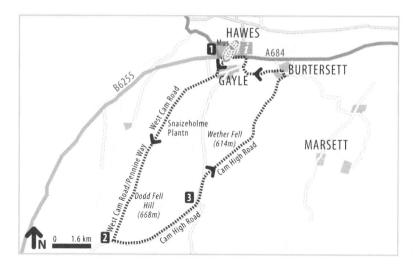

②   At that point there is a signpost indicating 'Horton 8 miles, Hawes 5 miles'. From here the Three Peaks – Whernside, Ingleborough and Pen-y-Ghent, backed by Fountains Fell – look magnificent. Turn left, leaving the Pennine Way, along Cam High Rd for 2½ miles to join the Hawes–Kettlewell road and continue along it for ½ mile. Just before the road descends, go right along walled Cam High Rd for 2 miles across the side of Drumaldrace and Wether Fell.

③   At a signpost 'Gayle 1½ miles' cross a wall stile on your left and go straight ahead, over the brow of the fell, on a curving path downhill to a facing stone wall with no stile. Climb over the wall and continue along a clear path, through a gateway near a hut. Keep on this meandering track for 2 miles to Burtersett. Once in the hamlet, turn right in front of Meadow Cottage, then turn left down the street, passing, on your right, Hillway Hall. Turn left just beyond the Methodist Chapel and take the path through a gated stile and across fields to Hawes. The way is paved with sandstone flags and is easy to follow. It brings you, via Old Gayle La, to the A684 just beyond the Wensleydale Press. Turn left along the A684 into Hawes.

Rivelin Valley

START The fishing pond car park (free), Rivelin Valley Rd, Sheffield, S6 5FE (immediately off Rivelin Valley Rd (A6101), to the south of Malin Bridge), GR 322883

DISTANCE short route 4 miles (6.5km); long route 5½ miles (9km)

SUMMARY Leisurely; mostly flat track and one gentle ascent and descent

MAPS OS Explorer 278 Sheffield & Barnsley; OS Landranger 110 Sheffield & Huddersfield

WHERE TO EAT AND DRINK the Rivelin Valley Café is economical; there are public toilets near the café

A wooded river valley track, then up to open fields with great views of Rivelin Valley.

1   Leave the car park on a path with the fishing pond on your left, continuing on the path until you reach a road. Turn right on a pavement then right again at the next junction. Go over a bridge, then cross the road and keep ahead to go down and along the riverside path to a café. After the café bear right (passing a playground on your right) and continue ahead to a footbridge over a river. Cross it and follow the main riverside path (the start of the Rivelin Nature Trail) until it emerges onto Rivelin Valley Rd at a double bend. Cross it and descend some steps to rejoin the path along the river. Follow the path along the valley to a footbridge. Cross it, then take the path to the left of the pond; continue for a while until you reach a footbridge over the river on your left.

2   For the shorter 4-mile route, turn left over this footbridge and go ahead uphill through two fields. Do not cross the stile but turn left to join the longer route past Windle House Farm (see 4, below). For the longer route ignore both this footbridge and the next, continuing along the path by the river until eventually you reach a stone arch footbridge on your left.

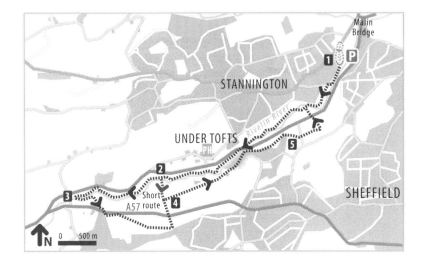

③   Cross this bridge and turn left, following the wide path as it climbs to meet the A57. Cross it and take the bridleway on the left (Coppice Rd). Follow this uphill until you reach some stone gateposts and a fingerpost on the left. Here, turn left over a stile and go back down to the A57 and recross. Continue down the path opposite through two fields and over a stile.

④   Turn right immediately and keep ahead, passing Windle House Farm, and continue along Long La. Immediately after a small parking area on the left, turn left onto a permissive bridleway heading downhill. Just before the road, turn right uphill, then go left at the next fork. Continue ahead over a stile and across three fields. At the end of these, go over a stile and continue straight ahead until you reach a road (Hagg Hill).

⑤   Turn right uphill for a short distance, then cross the road and continue ahead between allotments into a wood. Climb some steps and at a crossing of paths turn left (path becomes indistinct) down for a short distance through the trees to return back to Rivelin Valley Rd. Cross it and take the path slightly to the left down between the old allotments. Turn right at the end to rejoin the outgoing riverside route, and retrace your steps past the café to the starting point.

Whirlowbrook Hall to Ecclesall Wood

START Whirlowbrook Hall car park (free), Ecclesall Rd S, Sheffield S11 9QD, GR 307830

DISTANCE 4½ miles (7km)

SUMMARY Leisurely; mostly woodland tracks and gentle slopes

MAPS OS Explorer 278 Sheffield & Barnsley; OS Landranger 110 Sheffield & Huddersfield

WHERE TO EAT AND DRINK
The Woodland Discovery Centre (T0114-2356348) is open Fri, Sat and Sun for drinks and snacks

USEFUL WEBSITE
www.friendsofecclesallwoods.org.uk

A leisurely walk through parkland and woodland, passing a miniature railway, ponds and a remarkable old quarry.

[1] Behind Whirlowbrook Hall take the path on the left of the car park into woods. Turn immediately left, keeping left to follow an indistinct boundary path. At a path junction turn right to go over a stile, leaving the woods to follow the path bearing right (with Moorview Farm on your left). Go over the stile ahead and continue along the field boundary and over a ladder stile at the end. Go diagonally left to the far field boundary (with a farm on your right) through a stile in the boundary wall. Go straight ahead along the track to Hathersage Rd.

[2] Cross and walk down Ash House La, turning right at the end for a short distance along Limb La to follow an old walled track on the left (signed) down into woodland. Follow the path down, bearing right (follow signs to Abbeydale Rd South), past a house on the left, then bearing right downhill along Limb Brook. As the path approaches Abbeydale Rd you pass a miniature railway on your left (on the other side of the brook).

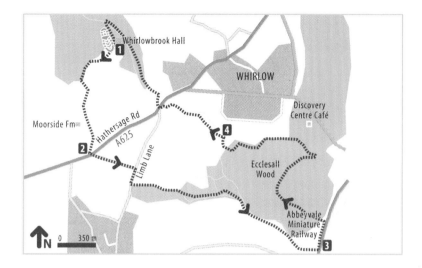

[3] When you reach Abbeydale Rd, turn left on a grassy area and re-enter the wood at the first footpath on your left. Take the path that bears right (signed to Abbey La), unless you would like better views of the site of the remarkable miniature railway, in which case retrace your steps. At the path junction go ahead to the next fingerpost and follow the sign bearing left to Abbey La. At the next junction bear right (signed Abbey La) to skirt the bird sanctuary on your left. Stay on the track, turn down left on a short, narrow surfaced path and turn left again at the bottom. Continue to a second set of fingerposts where (unless you wish to visit the Woodland Discovery Centre/café, in which case follow the signs and retrace your steps) you continue uphill on a wide track. At a path junction bear right through a gate and at the next gate/junction bear right down steps to go over a footbridge. Bear right again, leaving the wood through a gap in the stone wall.

[4] Keep right ahead along a sports field boundary. At a gap between conifer trees turn right into woodland and bear left along a path parallel to a stream. Follow the path to return to the sports field and exit ahead to cross Hathersage Rd. Return to the entrance to Whirlow Brook Park but go past it and look out for a fingerpost on your left just after some houses. Turn up here along a path to the back of a house and continue, passing a pond to eventually come to a wide path junction. Turn left here to go over the bridge and return to the car park.

Cannon Hall to Cawthorne

START Cannon Hall Country
Park car park (pay & display),
Bark House Lane, Cawthorne,
Barnsley S75 4AT, GR 273079

DISTANCE 5 miles (8km)

SUMMARY Leisurely; field paths
and tracks (gentle slopes)

MAPS OS Explorer OL1 The Peak
District: Dark Peak Area, and 278
Sheffield & Barnsley; OS Landranger
110 Sheffield & Huddersfield

WHERE TO EAT AND DRINK
The Spencer Arms
(www.spencerarms.co.uk),
or the more economical Cannon Hall
Tea Room (www.cannonhallfarm.
co.uk), both in Cawthorne

USEFUL WEBSITE
www.cannon-hall.co.uk

A delightful walk through rolling countryside, encompassing the eighteenth-century Cannon Hall, its park and museum, great views and attractive villages.

① From the car park head uphill, passing a small café on the left. Follow a fingerpost right to the farm café. In front of the café turn left to follow a path, passing several car parks to reach the main road. Turn right, continuing along the road over the crest of the hill to follow a fingerpost on the right. Cross the field, bearing slightly left, to a stile on the opposite side. Go over the stile and turn right, following the hedge towards the back of Cannon Hall Farm.

② Just before the fencing ahead, turn sharp left, heading downhill along a fence to trees to reach a gate alongside a wood. Go through it and continue ahead down past a pond and up to Dean Hill. Pass the farmhouse on your left, then go up a track to follow the field boundary wall on your left to another stile. Cross through a wood, bearing slightly right across a field to a stile and road. Turn right up the road into High Hoyland.

③ At a fingerpost on the right, go over a stile and head straight downhill to another stile into woodland. Bear right and follow a wide

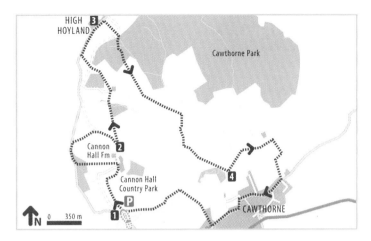

grassy track until you leave the wood over a stile. Go straight across the field and then the next one as far as the power lines. Here, bear left, following the power lines to the next stile, and bear right through the next field down to the corner to pass over a stream and up the track. Go over a stile in the wall ahead and continue down a path (following yellow signs).

4️⃣ At the bottom, turn left. With a brook to your right, keep left to go over a footbridge and turn left, following the brook now on your left, to another footbridge. Turn right (following a sign to Kexbrough), with the brook on your right. Go past a farm on your left, along drive to bear right over bridge and up track to turn right at the top along Darton Rd, into the centre of Cawthorne village. Continue ahead down Hill Top, past the museum and along Taylor Hill and Tivy Dale, until you reach the Park on the right. Turn right into this road and follow it as it eventually becomes a track leading into Cannon Hall Country Park. Head down to and across the bridge, then left along the brook and diagonally right to the car park.

Points of interest

Cannon Hall contains a museum, gardens, farm and country park.

Surprise View

START Surprise View car park
(pay & display) adjoining A6187,
S11 7TY (nearby), GR 252801

DISTANCE 5 miles (8km)

SUMMARY Moderate;
some rocky ascents

MAPS OS Explorer OL1
The Peak District: Dark Peak
Area; OS Landranger 110
Sheffield & Huddersfield

WHERE TO EAT AND DRINK
The Fox House (T01433-630374,
www.vintageinn.co.uk) and
National Trust café (T01433-
637904), both at Longshaw

Moorland and valley paths, a wooded gorge and an Iron Age hill fort, all with
great, extensive views.

① Leave Surprise View car park through the gate opposite the main
entrance. Climb up a path through woodland and then continue up,
picking your way through the grit stone boulders and keeping on until
you reach the prominent Mother Cap Stone ahead. Now bear right
along a footpath and continue to the rocks ahead. Here, bear slightly
right, passing the main rocks, going straight ahead to the edge to find
a steep rock path down. Follow the path along the ridge, ignoring
paths to left and right, making your way towards the left of Higger Tor
ahead, but look out for a fork in the path as you approach the rock
face. Take the right-hand path (ill-defined in summer due to bracken);
the left path takes you around to the opposite side of Higger Tor.

② Follow the path as it runs parallel to the Higger Tor rock face.
Turn right and follow the path below the rocks (ignore the first path
junction) but turn right on the next wide path, keeping right down
towards Carl Wark (or climb Higger Tor and return to this point).
Follow the path to just below Carl Wark. Skirt left on a path around
the edge of Carl Wark (an ill-defined path to the right is much drier)
and then head down towards the right-hand corner of the tree

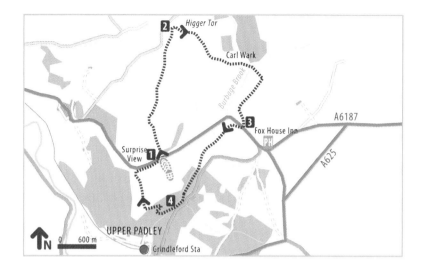

plantation below. Cross two bridges, then go up the steps to take the right fork uphill and turn right on a wide track. Follow this track to cross Hathersage Rd.

③ Go through the gate opposite and immediately turn right (a wall is on your right). Go down through a gate, turning right onto a rocky path (over a stream) and then immediately left. Go over the bridge at the bottom and turn left following Burbage Brook. Continue with the brook on your left. Eventually, take the rocky woodland path ahead through Padley Gorge. After a while, look out for a fingerpost on your right, signed for Surprise View and Bolehill.

④ Turn right and follow this woodland path uphill, but when it turns left, take the sharp right fork up a wide grassy ledge below rocks and go through a gate at the top. Turn left. Keep the stone wall on your left and follow the wall; as it bears right Mother Cap Stone soon comes into view ahead. Go through the gate ahead and along a grassy track as it winds its way to the top left-hand corner of the field. Do not go through the gate; instead, keep in the field and bear right for a short distance to go over a stile on the left. Cross Sheffield Rd to return to the car park.

Hebden Bridge

START St George's Square, Hebden
Bridge, HX7 8ET, GR 272993

DISTANCE 5½ miles (9km)

SUMMARY Moderate, but some
quite steep ascents and descents on
uneven paths (may be slippery when
wet) Maps OS Explorer OL21 South
Pennines; OS Landranger 104 Leeds
& Bradford, and 103 Blackburn &
Burnley

WHERE TO EAT AND DRINK
Marco's Café on Valley Rd (T01422-
649595) is excellent value for money

A walk that starts in Hebden Bridge's fascinating backstreets, continues along the
river up to moorland and farmland and returns through a delightful urban clough.

1 Start at St George's Square. Go along St George's St and over
a bridge to turn right along Valley Rd. Keep right to cross a bridge
and bear left along Victoria Rd, turning right up Windsor Rd until
you reach Windsor View on your left. Pass through a gap in the wall
opposite the end house, and down steps to turn right along a path
leading towards the river. With the river on your left, stay on this
path until you come to a junction, just after a bowling green, on the
opposite side of Hebden Water.

2 Cross left over Lee Mill Bridge and follow the track sharp right
to Upper Lea. Turn left, then soon right, taking a steep, stepped path
uphill to turn right onto a lane. Follow the lane and you will soon
join the Calderdale Way (continuing on this for a while). Shortly
afterwards, follow the path down, turning left at the bottom, passing
Midgehole Working Men's Club on your left. Go right over the bridge
and up to cross Midgehole Rd.

3 Turn right, then left, to continue uphill on the Calderdale Way
through the Pecket Well Clough, a National Trust wood; ignore paths
off the main track. You will eventually reach the A6033. Cross it and
go up the path opposite, turning right along Akroyd La. Passing
Shawcroft Farm on your left, take the next lane left – Shawcroft Hill.
Follow the Calderdale Way uphill until you reach Midgley Moor.

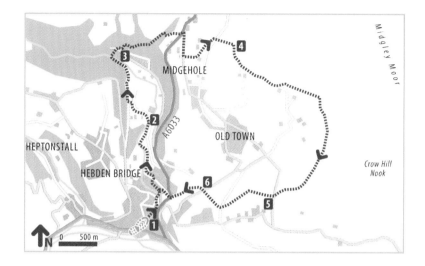

4 Turn right along the Way as it follows the boundary of farmland and moorland. After about 1½ miles look out for the edge of a golf course on your right (Crow Hill is over to your left, just ahead). Here, leave the moor and follow a stone wall on your right down to a kissing gate. Follow the path down, soon bearing left to a road. Take a rough path just to your left, which bears right to a stile beside a house.

5 Go over the stile and cross several fields following the yellow path markers ahead, ending in a short stretch skirting the garden of a house on your right. Stay ahead on a wide track (with Birchcliffe, a large housing estate, down to your left). Take the path opposite. Continue down on this path until you come to the end at a road (Sandy Gate).

6 Cross and take the path into Nutclough Wood. Follow the path down to a stone bridge. Turn left to follow the stream of Ibbot Royd Clough until you exit onto Keighley Rd (A6033). Cross this and go ahead along Foster La, but look out for a gap in the wall on the left. Here, go down the steps, which will lead you to Victoria Rd. Retrace your steps to the start.

START Digley Reservoir south
car park (free), Fieldhead Lane,
Holme, HD9 2QJ, GR 109077

DISTANCE 5½ miles (9km)

SUMMARY Moderate, but quite
hilly and some uneven paths

MAPS OS Explorer OL1
The Peak District: Dark Peak
Area; OS Landranger 110
Sheffield & Huddersfield

WHERE TO EAT AND DRINK
The Fleece Inn, Holme
(www.fleeceinnholme.co.uk),
and plenty of pubs and cafés
in nearby Holmfirth.

A lovely walk above reservoirs and through woodland: great views of an area
associated with *Last of the Summer Wine*.

[1] From the car park go through the gate at the end and follow the
path above the southern side of the reservoir. Go down some rough
steps and across Bilberry Reservoir dam. Turn left uphill and then
right, following the track and footpaths round the northern side of the
reservoir to a car park.

[2] Turn right through a gate, go down some steps and along a path
to emerge onto the road by Digley Dam. Join the road, cross the
junction, head downhill and go through a small gate on the right.
Follow the path down through trees to the bottom right corner to join
a metalled roadway. Turn left and walk to the A6024 in Holmbridge.
Turn right across the bridge over the River Holme and then left along
a road (signposted to a picnic area). Keep right at a junction and
continue up the steep Bank La.

[3] As Bank La becomes Brownhill La, turn left at a footpath sign
and head up the roadway to go through a garden gate to the right of
house no. 21A. Continue uphill with a stream on your right. At a stile
on the left bear right along a wooded clough. Cross a wall, turn right,

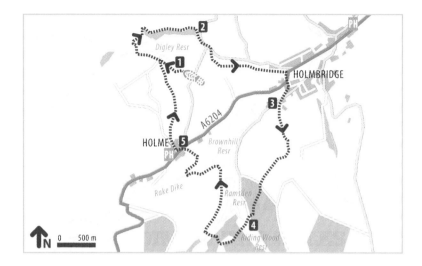

over the stream, and go left, skirting a field to reach a stone stile and gate. Turn right along a track, which soon becomes a path, and keep ahead to reach and cross a stile at the corner of a wood. Turn sharp left on a path up to a track and turn right downhill to the bottom.

④ Here, turn left, passing houses to cross the dam of Riding Wood Reservoir and follow the lane to a stile on the right (opposite the gated entrance to Yateholme Reservoir). Cross the stone stile, and walk straight downhill between trees to go through a gap in the wall at the bottom. Turn left and cross the footbridge below. Go right uphill above the stream, keeping right above and along Ramsden Reservoir. Follow the path as it goes uphill and through a gap in the wall, and then turn right downhill. At the path junction turn left and soon you will enter a valley, crossing a footbridge by a waterfall and then continuing up the opposite side to enter a field. Bear left, uphill, over two stone stiles, taking you left up to the road at Holme.

⑤ Turn left going past the access into Fieldhead La and turn right over cobbles. Go along Meal Hill Rd, bearing right. At a bend go through a gate on the right to follow the trodden path (Kirklees Way) over several stiles, eventually bearing right. Turn right to rejoin the path to the car park.

Brontë Country

START St Michael's Church,
Haworth, BD22 8DR, GR029373

DISTANCE 6 miles (10km)

SUMMARY Mostly paths
and tracks, but a short steep
climb up a grassy hillside

MAPS OS Explorer OL21;
OS Landranger 104 Leeds & Bradford

WHERE TO EAT AND DRINK
Cobbles & Clay Café, 60 Main St
(open daily, reasonable prices);
Haworth Old Hall Inn, Sun St
(bottom of Main St),
www.hawortholdhall.co.uk

Paths with extensive views of open moorland and farmland, followed by winding
lanes and ginnels through Haworth's heritage.

1   With the church tower on your left, follow the path and go
through the kissing gate onto a paved path. At the first turning right,
go up a narrow lane to a minor road. Cross it and take the path on
the left up into Penistone Country Park. At the signpost keep going
straight up, but soon take the path right to the trig point, which
should be just visible. From the point, turn sharp right down to the
Brontë Way, turning left along it and enjoying the views.

2   Staying on the Way, turn right at a signpost to Brontë Falls and
Top Withens. Cross a road onto the path opposite, turning left and
following a track along the valley. Eventually the valley becomes
narrow and wooded, and quite rocky as you descend to the Falls.
(Here, do not cross the bridge unless you wish to visit Top Withens
and then return to this point.)

3   At the bridge, turn left up the steep hillside path alongside
the Falls (not signposted but just visible). At the summit the path
becomes paved. On reaching Harbour Lodge, follow the signpost left
to Haworth along a wide track. Continue until you come to signposts.
Follow the path down to the right towards Leeshaw Reservoir. At the
bottom turn left along a wall, and then take the path signposted right.

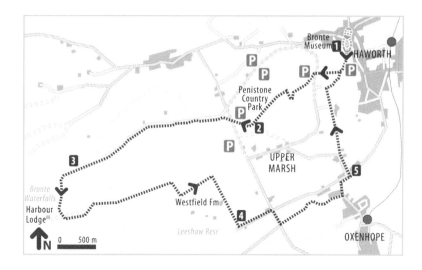

This takes you down to a road, passing Westfield Farm on your right.

④ Turn left, and then right, down Moorside La. Follow the track (signpost on your left) to Pin Hill End Farm. Go straight ahead along a double-walled ginnel, over a stile, and take the left of the two stiles in front of you around an old house. At the end bear left through a ginnel in front of some cottages and through a metal kissing gate to an old path. At the end turn right into a lane and bear left behind cottages and through a gate. Cross a field and go along the road, turning left at the end, up Moorhouse La to Marsh La.

⑤ Turn right and take the first left up Old Oxenhope La. At the bend turn right (signposted) by the side of the farm gate and follow the wall left. Continue to field junctions, carry on ahead but with the wall on your right, and go through a narrow gate at the end. Follow the path round and cross a road, taking the path ahead through two fields. Go through the gate at the end onto an old walled track around Sowdens Farm. This brings you back to the path where you began. Continue ahead to the church.

Hooton Pagnell

START All Saints Church, B6422
(Elmsall La), Hooton Pagnell,
DN5 7BW, GR 486080

DISTANCE 6 miles (10km)

SUMMARY Leisurely; farmland
path and track and gentle hills

MAPS OS Explorer 278
Sheffield & Barnsley & 279
Doncaster; OS Landranger 111
Sheffield & Doncaster

WHERE TO EAT AND DRINK
Unfortunately, quite a distance
away at Brodsworth Hall (entrance
fee) or Marr village (pub)

A pleasant walk from an attractive historic village, following many very old paths
through farmland and woodland.

1⃞ From the church (on the main road) walk past the entrance to
Hooton Pagnell Hall. Cross the stile on the opposite side of the road
and walk down the stone steps. Walk straight ahead to a small group
of trees, passing through them, and follow the path/signs ahead to a
road (you may prefer to walk along the field boundaries).

2⃞ At the road turn right and continue, passing a narrow private
lane on the left (once a railway line), to shortly go left over a stile at a
footpath (signed). Follow the track towards Hooton Pagnell Woods.
Skirt around to the left of the woods, following the path ahead as you
leave the woods to cross fields, and eventually reaching Elmsall La.

3⃞ Turn left and then shortly right to climb up to a path that was
once the Frickley Railway. Continue along the disused railway path,
but just after some overhead lines (before a bridge) turn right off the
track and take a path to the left of Moorhouse Grange Farm. Skirt
around the farm to Moorhouse La.

4⃞ Turn left along the lane, passing the signed path on the right, and
continue until just after Gap Farm (the Equestrian Centre). Here, turn
right up the track (Stanwell La), and continue up to the top to cross

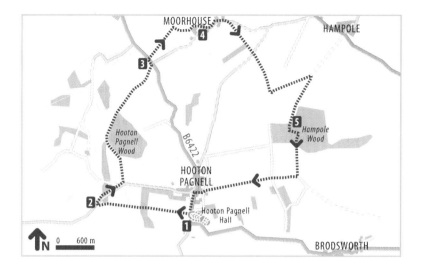

North Field Rd. Continue up the hill to a fingerpost, where you turn left towards Hampole. When you meet a track, turn sharp right up the track to the right of Hampole Wood.

⑤   At the wood, enter at the gate and go ahead. At a junction turn left, slightly uphill. Just past an open area, take the narrow footpath on the right (signed), between trees. At the stile take the track left to Rat Hall Farm. Pass the farmhouse and immediately turn right, going alongside a field to enter the enclosed lane, Narrow Balk. At its end, turn left and quickly right along a footpath between houses to reach the B6442 road in Hooton Pagnell. Turn left to return to the church.

Points of interest

Information about All Saints Church and Hooton Pagnell Hall – and the owners of the Hall who 'dominated the community for centuries' – can be found on the following websites: www.hootonpagnell.com and www. doncasterfhs.co.uk/content/hooton-pagnell.

Nearby Brodsworth Hall and grounds (English Heritage) are definitely worth a visit: www.english-heritage.org.uk/daysout/properties/brodsworth-hall-and-gardens/.

START Langsett Barn car park (free), Langsett, S36 4GY, GR 210004

DISTANCE 6½ miles (10.5km)

SUMMARY Moderate; flat track around reservoir, but uneven and steepish paths on moors

MAPS OS Explorer OL1 The Peak District: Dark Peak Area; OS Landranger 110 Sheffield & Huddersfield

WHERE TO EAT AND DRINK
The Bank View Café (T01226-762337, www.bankviewcafe.co.uk) and The Wagon and Horses pub (www.langsettinn.com), both in Langsett

A lovely walk around the reservoir, returning on higher moorland and woodland paths with splendid views.

[1]   From the far corner of the car park take the path down, turning right at the bottom along the reservoir track. When the track ends, turn up right and continue ahead along a bridleway. When this track bends to the right, turn left down onto the Pennine Bridleway signposted to Swinden. At the fork, turn left, following a path to a stone barn on the right. Immediately after the barn turn right, then soon go through a gate on your left into a wood. Follow this path as it descends to a wall. Here, turn right, then continue on the path as it turns sharply left downhill and go through a gate.

[2]   Immediately turn left uphill by a fence, with the wood on your left and a wall on your right. Continue along the path above the River Little Don, eventually re-entering the wood through a gate on the left. Soon afterwards, bear left onto a path heading left above a brook to a footbridge. Cross and soon turn right onto a track heading downhill to cross a stone bridge (Brookhouse Bridge). Turn left and follow the well-used path as it winds around, first to the right then left uphill, before heading straight ahead past Hingcliff Hill (to your right) to a marker post.

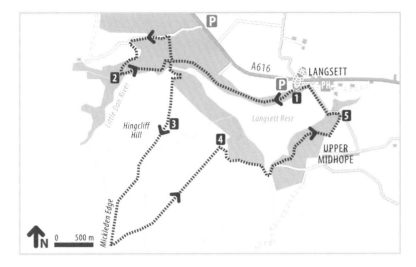

③ Here, you can carry on straight ahead uphill, but the path underfoot becomes uneven and may be muddy. (Alternatively, for a shorter walk you can turn left and follow the path gently downhill to the ruin that was once North America Farm. Go through the gate to rejoin the route at ④, below.) Otherwise continue uphill; the path eventually descends and heads into a valley at Mickleden. Continue along the edge of the valley until you reach a marker post on the left. Turn left and stay on this path, as it soon descends giving good views along the Don Valley. Eventually you reach a wall running parallel to the left. Follow this down to a track with a gate on the left and a ruin beyond it.

④ Turn right along the track leading down to the reservoir, over a bridge and, soon, through a gate. Keep left along the reservoir and enter woodland on Yorkshire Water's permissive path. Eventually follow a sign to bear right uphill, keeping ahead at the top of the bank (wall on your right) to exit the woodland at a gate. Turn left and left again at the road.

⑤ Follow the road down and follow the reservoir wall. At the end of the wall turn left on a path through a gate and soon head uphill to return to the car park.

Whirlowbrook Park & Porter Valley

START Whirlowbrook Hall car park (free), Ecclesall Rd S, Sheffield, S11 9QD, GR 307830

DISTANCE 6½ miles (10.5km)

SUMMARY Moderate; wooded valley and open fields with some steep short sections

MAPS OS Explorer 278 Sheffield & Barnsley; OS Landranger 110 Sheffield & Huddersfield

WHERE TO EAT AND DRINK There are two cafés and the Norfolk Arms (www.norfolkarms.com) en route and lots of excellent cafés just off the route on Sheffield's Sharrow Vale Rd

A walk from Whirlowbrook, through lovely woodland, a landscaped garden and fields, and returning along the fascinating Porter Valley.

1 From the second car park, behind Whirlowbrook Hall, take the footpath (initially paved) into the woodland on the right. Follow the path down over a bridge and at a path junction turn left to a fingerpost turning up a steep path on the right. Go over two stiles ahead, then turn left and soon turn right over another stile. With a wall on your left, continue ahead through three fields to Wigley Farm and Ringinglow Rd.

2 Cross, turn left at a footpath sign and go over a stone stile on the right, following a path right along a hedge/fence to the end and turning right between trees and some fencing. At Cottage La cross over and go ahead along Common La (track) through a park to another road. Turn left, and go along the road around a bend, but at the next bend follow a footpath right beside stone building to pick up an old paved track uphill to houses (Trapp La). Continue to a junction, and follow a fingerpost on the left down some steps, following a path/track bearing right into woodland.

3 Take the second path on the left, downhill. At the bottom go over the bridge/stile, straight across the field ahead, then follow a sign right along a field boundary to enter woodland. The path bears left down

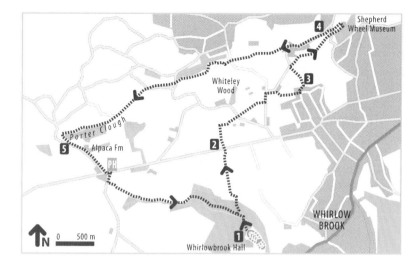

to a track along the Porter Brook; turn right here. Keep straight on to cross a road. Follow the paved lane bearing right, continuing along Porter Brook to the Shepherd Wheel Museum on your left. Go left to the back of the museum and along the millpond. Bear right to go up to Hangingwater Rd and cross.

4 Take the right surfaced track and continue to cross Whitely Wood Rd and left to follow the path ahead (with the brook on your right) to Ivy Cottage La. Turn left following the lane right to Forge Dam Café/toilets. Go up the slope to the dam and bear right around the dam, go over the bridge and turn right on the path. Cross the road ahead and continue, bearing right to cross another junction. Continue on the right path ahead to the end, turning right to join a cycle path (keeping right ahead). Cross another road to enter Porter Clough and continue on into the wood. Go left after the third wooden footbridge and up to a car park and Fulwood Rd.

5 Turn left along the road (passing Alpaca Farm) to the end. Turn left to cross the road at the Norfolk Arms. Go along Sheephill Rd, turning left at a fingerpost to Limb Valley. Follow the path ahead, ignoring two fingerposts to the right; turn right at the third sign down some steps into woodland. Stay on this path until you reach the bridge at the beginning of the walk, where you turn right to retrace your steps to the car park.

START Saltaire (outside Salts
Mill, bottom of Victoria Rd),
BD18 3LF, GR 139381

DISTANCE 7 miles (11km)

SUMMARY Moderate; gentle rocky
climb up Shipley Glen, otherwise
paths, tracks and a few quiet lanes

MAPS OS Explorer 288 Bradford
& Huddersfield; OS Landranger
104 Leeds & Bradford

WHERE TO EAT AND DRINK
The Five Rise Locks Café, Leeds
and Liverpool Canal (T01274-
569664, www.fiveriselockscafe.
co.uk); The Half Moon Café, Roberts
Park, Saltaire (T01274-594707,
www.halfmooncafe.co.uk/)

This walk encompasses the World Heritage Site of Saltaire, a beautiful wooded
glen and a fascinating stretch of canal.

1 .Cross the bridges over the canal and river at the end of Victoria
Rd and turn sharp left to walk alongside the river, bearing slightly
right and passing the Cricket Clubhouse. Go through the gate on your
left onto a grassy area. Keep ahead, but when you come to a footbridge
on your left, turn right up between houses. Cross two roads ahead,
then bear slightly left up a path to a woodland. At the junction turn
left through the woodland on an easy wide path; at the fork, turn left
up Shipley Glen.

2 Keep straight on, and where the path divides keep right on a
rocky path, which eventually emerges at the top of the Glen. Keep left
in this open area, passing a car park (off Glen Rd). When you reach
a signpost, turn left down a path to a bridge and cross the beck. With
the beck on your right, walk forward on Saltaire Rd until you reach
the busy Otley Rd.

3 Cross the road, turn right, and then take the first left (The
Green). Continue, passing the Acorn Inn, and eventually you come
to a junction where you leave the road (which bears sharp right and

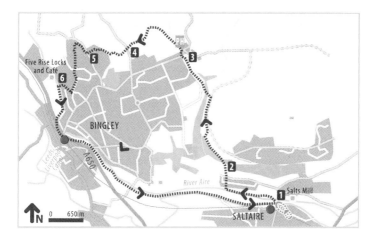

becomes a drive to the Old Corn Mill). Instead of following the road, go up the overgrown track on your left. You soon pass a reservoir on your right. Turn left past a house (onto Tewitt La), ultimately reaching a road by Lower Heights Farm.

4 Cross the road, turn left and follow the sign pointing right towards a stone house. Go towards the house, but then turn right of the building and go over a stone stile in the wall. Go straight ahead across the field towards the far right-hand corner. Cross the stone stile and walk straight ahead by the wall side for two fields. Cross a stone stile on the left and go to the right of a house. Go down to a mini roundabout and bear right to reach a main road.

5 Turn right along the road past Greenhill Crag Farm. Cross the road and turn left at the footpath sign ahead into woodland. Follow the path downhill to reach a road. Cross and walk down Pinedale to where the path continues down, then turn right along Beck La. Continue forward, passing allotments on the left.

6 Turn left at the roundabout and cross over the Leeds–Liverpool Canal – or call at the Five Rise Locks Café. Turn left and walk back along the towpath, passing the Five Rise Locks. Follow the canal back to Saltaire and the Victoria Rd bridge.

START Union Street South car park (pay & display), off A646, Todmorden, OL14 5QE, GR 93762409

MAPS OS Explorer OL21 South Pennines; OS Landranger 103 Blackburn & Burnley

DISTANCE 7 miles (11km)

SUMMARY Quite a tough walk; a few steep uphill and downhill paths, but mostly tracks and paths

WHERE TO EAT AND DRINK Good choice of pubs and cafés in Todmorden

Splendid industrial heritage, surrounded by spectacular steep-sided hills with great views.

[1] From the car park, turn right along the canal towpath to the Rochdale Rd bridge. Pass below and cross it to continue on the opposite bank. Pass a series of locks and go under an impressive railway bridge before going under a road bridge at Gauxholme. Cross at Lock 24 and turn right to cross the road.

[2] Walk straight ahead uphill along Pexwood Rd. There are excellent views before you reach a junction at the top. Turn left along Stones Rd, soon turning sharp right and passing Lob Quarry on the left. At the end of the road turn right onto Calderdale Way.

[3] When you reach open fields, just past a house on your right, bear left uphill to a stone wall. Follow the wall to a lane – Parkin La (here you have a view of Stoodley Pike). Turn left along the lane and at the bend turn sharp right along a track to follow the Calderdale Way off to the right between buildings, downhill to woodland (caution – the path has eroded as you enter the woodland). Continue down the steep descent to a lane at the bottom.

[4] Turn left on the lane and continue down past the Leisure Centre to the bottom. Turn left along Burnley Rd and cross when safe to re-join The Way (signed) on the opposite side, at Stoney Royd La.

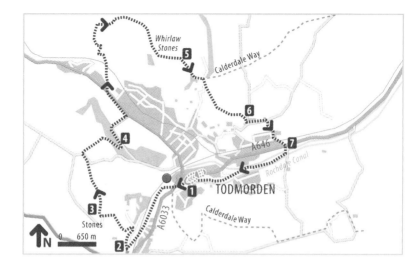

There is a very long, steep climb up the lane to the very top of the hill, passing an isolated farm to reach a track junction. Turn right, bearing left below Whirlaw Stones to a gate and a surfaced track.

⑤ Follow the track downhill. Look out for the Calderdale Way joining the track from the right, and at the next bend over a stream take the left path (signed) uphill, leaving the track. Stay on this path (leaving the Way as it goes off to the left) as it skirts the golf course, passing the clubhouse and car park to reach Hey Head La.

⑥ Here, turn right downhill and left at a T-junction. At the end of the cemetery (on your left) turn sharp right (fingerpost), then left after a cottage down some steps, and immediately before the next cottage turn right downhill. At the next path junction turn left. On emerging between stone cottages, turn left, then soon right onto a road of semi-detached houses (Castle La). Turn left at the next road junction, and follow the road down into the No Entry section. Emerge on the A646. Turn left and shortly cross over.

⑦ Turn right down Woodhouse La (signed Youth Hostel). Cross the River Calder and take the steps on the left down to the canal. Turn right and follow the canal back to Todmorden and the start.

WALK

92

Cordwell Valley

START Totley Hall Lane junction with Baslow Rd, S17 4AA, GR 308796

DISTANCE 7 miles (11km)

SUMMARY Moderate; some quite long ascents/descents and difficult stiles

MAPS: OS Explorer OL24; OS Landranger 110 Sheffield & Huddersfield

WHERE TO EAT AND DRINK Good pubs at Totley, Holmesfield and one at Millthorpe

A delightful walk through woodland and fields of the Cordwell Valley, passing some of the ancient halls in this area. Lots of great views.

① From Baslow Rd, walk to the end of Totley Hall La. Go over a stile by the gate ahead and keep left across two fields. Keep ahead to Gillfield Wood and bear left downhill to cross a bridge over Totley Brook. Follow a path up to woodland to skirt around the first hall, Woodthorpe Hall (best viewed from the lane).

② Turn right along the lane and, when the lane bends right, join the path going straight ahead into Holmesfield Park Wood. Follow the waymarks for 1 mile, and continue ahead to join the lane into Holmesfield village. Cross the road by the Angel Inn. Follow the fingerpost by the side of the George and Dragon Inn, into Cordwell Valley. Continue down to a stile and a footbridge, on the left, towards the hamlet of Cartledge. Climb up the field to reach the road. Turn left and first right.

③ Go along the lane, passing Cartledge Hall, and take the track through Cartledge Hall Farm. Keep ahead, then bear right into a field, continuing down on the left, over a stile and passing a bungalow to join the road. Turn left into Millthorpe. Cross at the junction into Mill La. Go up to a cobblestoned area and take the field path over the stile keeping left, but bearing right at the next field to cross bridge over Pingle Dyke. Take the path right to enter Rose Wood. Follow the right-hand path uphill, and go right at the next junction along a woodland path, over a bridge and through trees to a gate.

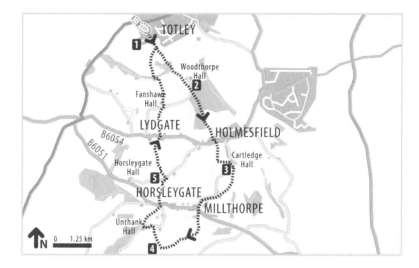

④ Leave Rose Wood, keeping ahead until you reach Unthank La. Turn left up to Unthank Hall. Take a footpath on the right through a field, following the wall down to the right and over the stile (at the second gate). Follow the hedge as it descends. Immediately into second field, climb down to cross stile and right to lane. Turn left, and cross at the junction to follow the bridleway up to Horsleygate La.

⑤ Turn right to Horsleygate (the hall is left). Turn left at the fingerpost pointing to Lydgate. Go up, crossing two fields and going through a gap on the right of the second field. Turn left and right over a stile into a large field. Turn left uphill over a stile, and go across the track and through a gate. Now bear right towards a farmhouse and a stone stile onto the B6054. Cross over, and after Lydgate Cottage go left to Fanshawe Gate. Follow the field boundary, but where it turns right take a path left to a lane. Turning right past the hall, follow a sign left, down to an exit through a gate. Go downhill to woods, over a brook and up, turning left on the main path. Take the next right over a stile onto a track and right again to retrace your route back to Totley.

WALK

93 Wentworth

START Main Street car park (pay & display), Wentworth (next to the Rockingham pub), S62 7TL, GR SK387982

DISTANCE 7 miles (11km)

SUMMARY Leisurely; mainly gently undulating terrain but one or two paths may be muddy

MAPS OS Explorer 278 Sheffield & Barnsley; OS Landranger 110 Sheffield & Huddersfield

WHERE TO EAT AND DRINK
The Rockingham Arms and the George and Dragon (www.georgeanddragonwentworth.co.uk) and two cafés in Wentworth village

This walk passes the magnificent Wentworth Woodhouse, its monuments and deer park, returning through the lovely village.

1 Leave the car park through a gate at the back and cross the playing field. Turn right onto Clayfield La, continuing to a road junction (Cortworth La), and turn left. Follow this road past the next junction (with Coaley La), turning left immediately after a bus stop into a drive to Cortworth House. Continue ahead through a kissing gate on the right, going uphill across fields to the hamlet of Street. Turn right and follow Street La to a wood, turning left through a gap in the wall up through the trees to Hoober Stand.

2 Immediately after Hoober Stand take the path on the right, down to a tree-lined path to regain Street La. Turn left and continue into Hoober and left again along Hoober La (B6090). Go past a farm and cross in front of some houses, taking the path on the left into woodland. Leave at a stile and cross the fields following the path to Low Stubbin. Here, turn right along Stubbin Rd (B6089) past the junction with Haugh Rd to the crest of the hill. Cross and continue down to a footpath sign between Prospect Cottage and Glebe House. Turn left onto this path to a field. Turn right and follow the old track round to the left as it runs downhill between trees to its end.

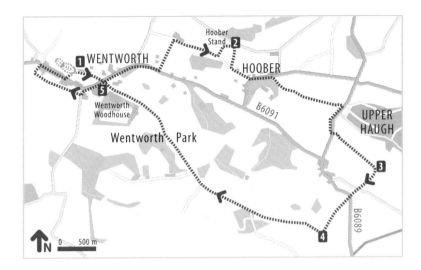

3 Turn right onto a cobbled path (Roman Ridge), then continue along a field boundary to a road junction. Go ahead on Rig La to the B6089. Cross and take the path opposite (also Roman Ridge) downhill to Mill Dam. (If the last part of the descent to Mill Dam is muddy, an alternative path is available through the trees to the left.)

4 Turn right (with Mill Dam on your left) onto the tarmacked track (a permissive footpath) along the reservoir, then go through a gate onto a roadway. Bear right along this road until Wentworth Woodhouse appears. Here, bear right at a fingerpost and follow the fence past the side of the house onto an access road. Follow this road past the impressive former eighteenth-century stables to the main road.

5 Turn left down to Hague La junction, then left again. Shortly afterwards cross Hague La to a gate on the right and continue along the track straight ahead to the church. At the church, turn right down to the main village street and then right again to return to the car park.

WALK

94

Worsbrough Country Park & Wentworth Castle

START Worsbrough Country Park car park (pay & display), off Park Rd (A61), Worsbrough, S70 5LJ, GR 352033

DISTANCE 7 miles (11km)

SUMMARY A leisurely walk through fields and parkland

MAPS OS Explorer 278 Sheffield & Barnsley; OS Landranger 110 Sheffield & Huddersfield

WHERE TO EAT AND DRINK Cafés at Worsbrough Mill Museum (www.worsbrough-mill.com) and Wentworth Castle (www.wentworthcastle.org); pubs nearby in Worsbrough village

A walk through a country park to Stainborough's historic (listed) parkland and castle.

1   From the car park follow the sign to the old corn mill museum/visitor centre. Pass right of the centre and pond and continue up to the reservoir. Follow the path along the left side of the reservoir. As the path ends, rejoin the main track on your left.

2   Turn right over a stone bridge, continuing ahead over wetland, then uphill to a junction. Turn left across open fields towards houses. At the hamlet, with Rockley Hall gate on your left, turn right up a lane to go over the M1. At the road junction ahead, turn right along the roadside. Eventually take the signed path over a stile on the opposite side of the road. Take the path diagonally left over a field to a cottage (and obelisk). Over the stile, go through a metal gate ahead and follow the path towards and then along a wall. After the next stile turn right through a gate into woodland to take the Parkland Trail left. Continue bearing left until you see the temple.

3   Here, go through a gate in the deer fence and turn left in front of the temple, following the path ahead and keeping the trees to your left. Turn left at the end of the trees skirting the woodland. After two gates (unless you wish to bear left to visit the statue in the woods), turn immediately right and go up a grassy tree-lined avenue to Wentworth Castle. (If you wish to visit the castle, garden or visitor centre, turn right through a gate and left to another gate – and then retrace your steps.)

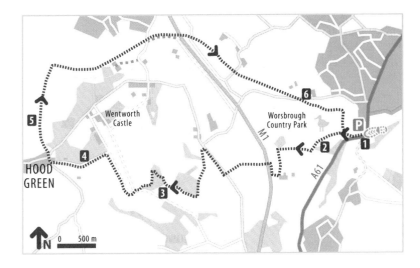

HOOD GREEN

0   500 m

4   From the end of the avenue follow the fence left around the house to a gate. Continue on a path, skirting the gardens, passing a pond on your left and a cottage on the right, until you reach the village of Hood Green. Carry on to a main road junction where you turn right, but soon cross to take a path on the left. Continue downhill over several fields, over a disused narrow-gauge rail track, bearing right to a footbridge and a stile.

5   Keep ahead up to and over a footbridge and shortly the path emerges onto a disused railway line, now the Dove Valley Trail. Turn right and follow the Trail, eventually crossing the M1, before coming to a car park on the left.

6   Here, cross the road ahead to regain the Trail. Then, as the reservoir comes into view on your right, bear right off the Trail onto a path down to the reservoir. Follow the signs back to the museum around the reservoir.

Points of interest

Wentworth Castle has a Grade1 Listed landscaped parkland and gardens, and a recently restored conservatory (www.wentworthcastle.org).

WALK

95 Totley Moor

START Fox House Inn car
park, Hathersage Rd (A6187),
Sheffield, S11 7TY, GR 267803

DISTANCE 7¾ miles (12.5km)

SUMMARY Moderate; mainly
moorland paths and tracks, with
one steep descent and ascent

MAPS OS Explorer OL1 The Peak
District: Dark Peak Area, and
OL24 The Peak District: White
Peak Area; OS Landranger 110
Sheffield & Huddersfield

WHERE TO EAT AND DRINK
The Fox House (T01433-630374,
www.vintageinn.co.uk) and
National Trust café (T01433-
637904), both at Longshaw

A walk through a National Trust estate and moorland, returning through a nature reserve. Splendid views of Peak Park.

1 From the car park cross Hathersage Rd by the bus stop and turn right. Go down to the road junction, cross over and turn right to a gate and fingerpost. Go through the gate and down to the access road to Longshaw Lodge, turning left along it. Just before the visitor centre turn left and follow a wide track as it bears right behind the Lodge through trees to exit through a gate. Turn right along a wide grassy track, and where it forks go left up to a road junction and cross straight ahead. Go through a gate and continue on the track to the isolated White Edge Lodge.

2 Just before the Lodge take a path on the left by a wall and head uphill to a gate on the top of White Edge. Go through, turn left then immediately right, continuing straight ahead over the moor. On reaching a road, turn right along it. Soon you will see a gate on the opposite side of the road, cross, go through it and follow the narrow path ahead across the moor. Take care as a section of this path can be boggy. Eventually you will reach a ruined wall. Turn right and follow it straight ahead, passing a trig point on your left, across two tracks until you reach an extremely large cairn.

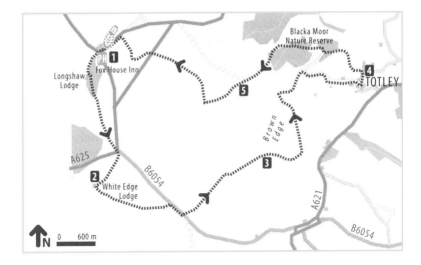

3 Continue ahead downhill, following the path as it eventually
bears left to a wall. Turn left along a path as it winds below Brown
Edge, eventually joining Moss Rd. Turn right onto this track, which
becomes tarmacked, and follow it downhill until it meets Lane Head
Rd. Turn left along it at the back of the sports ground to a road
junction.

4 Turn left into Strawberry Lee La and follow it round until it
reaches a small car parking area on the left. Go through a gate ahead
and continue along the path into Blacka Moor Nature Reserve. Follow
the path as it starts to climb, with a brook down to the left. At a
junction turn left and continue uphill to go through a gate in a wall.

5 Following the fingerpost signs to Longshaw, go straight ahead
onto a narrow, grassy path uphill, bearing to the left side of the
hill in front. Eventually go over a stile and through a gate, turning
right onto a grassy track. Follow this to a road (A625), cross and
continue through a gate on the path as it winds over the moor to join
Hathersage Rd (A6187). Turn left for a short distance downhill, then
cross to the car park.

Yorkshire Sculpture Park

START Visitor Centre car park
(pay & display), Yorkshire
Sculpture Park, Bretton Hall,
Bretton, WF4 4LG, GR 285128

DISTANCE 7¾ miles (12.5km)

SUMMARY Moderate; mainly field
and woodland tracks and paths, with
no prolonged ascents or descents

MAPS OS Explorer 278 Sheffield
& Barnsley and 288 Bradford &
Huddersfield; OS Landranger
110 Sheffield & Huddersfield

WHERE TO EAT AND DRINK There
are cafés and an excellent (and
popular) restaurant at the Sculpture
Park (www.ysp.co.uk); also for food try
the Cherry Tree pub at High Hoyland

A walk from the Sculpture Park through rolling countryside, climbing steadily up
to High Hoyland before returning.

1   From the Visitor Centre go downhill almost to the lake. Turn
right through a gate to the footbridge, go over, turning left alongside
the Lower Lake. At the dam turn right then right again, passing the
well. Take a stepped path left uphill. Continue along the ridge, passing
tree/wall artworks, until you eventually reach the metal cage.

2   Follow the path downhill through trees and join a track below
Longside Gallery. Turn right through a gate to join the path back
towards Bretton Hall, then turn left along a track up to a gatehouse.
Turn left along the road up to the next road junction, turning left and
continuing until you reach a fingerpost on the right.

3   Turn right and follow the path as it bears gradually right into
High Hoyland village. At the end turn left, following the road bearing
right, passing a public house to a road junction. Turn left downhill
along the road until you reach a fingerpost and gate on the right.

4   Follow the waymarked path, passing houses and walking through
trees to turn right at a path junction. Shortly go left over a stile, across
a field then through woodland, keeping left to skirt the back of a farm

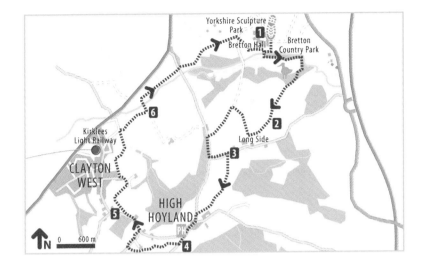

to a lane. Turn right along the lane up to a road junction. Turn left and follow this road downhill for a while until you reach a track on the right with a fingerpost.

⑤ Turn right onto the track, then sharp left over a stile. Continue ahead downhill across a field, over two stiles, then up to a path junction. Turn right along the left side of the hedge and over a stile. Pass allotments on your left and emerge on a lane to turn left. Follow the lane round to a house on the right, turning right along a path to a field. Bear right and eventually go right, through a kissing gate, into another field. Bear left, and at a kissing gate on the left go down through fields towards factories to turn right on a track. Go left at a junction, passing a factory, to emerge opposite a sewage works at the end.

⑥ Turn left along the lane, over the brook, to a stile on the right (in a hedge). Cross it and go ahead over three fields and three stiles to a lane. Cross into trees, following the path as it bears left to join a track. Turn right, follow it ahead then go left to and over a footbridge. Bear left on the uphill path to the top and continue over two fields to enter Bretton Country Park through a gate. Head uphill on the many paths to return, enjoying the works of art, as you head back towards the galleries, restaurants and car park.

97 Harden & St Ives

START Myrtle Park, Bingley, BD16 1HJ, GR 108388 Distance 8 miles (13km)

DISTANCE 8 miles (13km)

SUMMARY Moderate with a few rough paths; a steepish ascent and descent

MAPS OS Explorer 288 Bradford & Huddersfield; OS Landranger 104

WHERE TO EAT AND DRINK
The Malt Shovel Inn, Harden (T01535-272357); cafés in Myrtle Park and St Ives, and pubs in Bingley

A walk through farmland to the beautiful Goit Stock Valley and waterfalls, following paths within delightful parkland to an excellent viewpoint.

1   Enter Myrtle Park via Myrtle Court to follow a path left, crossing a footbridge over the River Aire. Walk along the enclosed path to a lane. Turn right to Beck Foot. Cross a footbridge on the right over the beck and go over two stiles to a lane. Before a house, turn left down steps and over a bridge. Cross Shipley golf course (carefully), bearing right and following white marker stones to cross a stile.

2   Bear left along a path to reach a wall stile. Cross and follow a rough track uphill through woodland, ignoring other paths until the main path forks. Take the narrower left fork uphill, following a fence to a stone stile. Cross the next field to a stile. Bear left to the corner of the next field and over a stile. An enclosed path turns right, then follows the wall to Lee La. To the left, pass through the left-hand of two gateways opposite, continuing ahead and following the field boundary wall to a stile.

3   Turn right, then follow a downhill path on the left; continue along a wooded valley. Exit through a gate on the left and cross Wilsden Rd (carefully) to the garden centre. Turn left then right on a path behind cottages. Continue on the path to some cottages at the end.

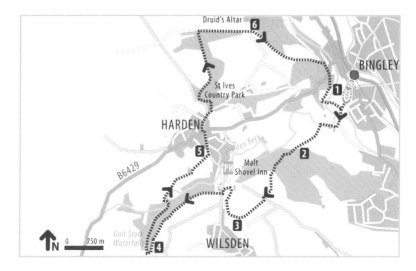

4 Turn right down a lane, turning right before a bridge on Goit Stock Way. Follow a stream on your left, passing a waterfall, to the end. At Valley Park turn sharp left over a footbridge and stay left to turn up a path (signed) on the right before some houses. Bear right and, just after passing Goit Stock cottages, take a path down into woodland on the right. Follow the path to pass a farm on the left, bearing left to rejoin Wilsden Rd.

5 Turn left to Harden. At the junction cross and turn right up Keighley Rd; turn right into the St Ives Estate. After a short distance along the drive, turn left up some steps to a T-junction. Turn left and follow the path as it bears right, passing Lady Blantyre's Rock, and then left by the side of woodland. Bear right at a junction, keeping to the edge of the trees and passing a golf course. Continue, to emerge onto Altar La. Turn right along the lane to a junction. Here, bear slightly left across Altar La and take a narrow path for 150yds across rough land to the Druid's Altar viewpoint.

6 Retrace your steps to Altar La and follow the lane down to Harden Rd. Cross over and take the narrow track opposite through woodland downhill to reach a field. At the end of the field cross the footbridge over the River Aire and bear left through Myrtle Park to return to the starting point.

98 Bradfield & Three Reservoirs

START The Sands car park (free), Lower Bradfield, S6 6LB, GR 262920

DISTANCE 8¼ miles (13.5km)

SUMMARY Moderate; mostly grassy paths and tracks with one steepish climb up to High Bradfield

MAPS OS Explorer OL1 The Peak District: Dark Peak Area; OS Landranger 110

WHERE TO EAT AND DRINK There are cafés in Low Bradfield, and popular pubs in Low and High Bradfield: The Plough (www.theploughlowbradfield.co.uk) and The Old Horns Inn (www.theoldhorns.co.uk) respectively

A delightful walk, taking in the heritage of the twin Bradfield villages, moorland edges, three reservoirs and attractive Pennine valleys.

1 At the car park entrance turn right, following a path along a stream (ignore the first footbridge on the right), and continue over the next footbridge, up steps and along a path to a road. Cross and take a path up through a gate. Carry on uphill across fields to steps on the left alongside a churchyard. Follow the path round and turn left through the main gate. Continue in front of the church, turn right and then left through the cemetery to its end. After a gate take the path ahead then left down through trees to go through a gate and continue left on a walled path.

2 Before a gate on the path, turn right then immediately left through a gateway, then right again uphill and soon left on a level grassy path (ignore the path uphill). Continue ahead on the path, over the next stile on the left, and bear right to a ladder stile. Cross, turning left to pass the ruined farm buildings of Rocher Head. Keep ahead to the gate and follow the track along a stream, then around to the left through a gate to reach and cross a road.

3 Go over a stile and ahead along the path, but soon bear left to a ladder stile. Go over, cross the road, going down through gates to follow a path, bearing left along a wall down to the edge of Agden Reservoir. Turn right and follow the track round over a stone bridge,

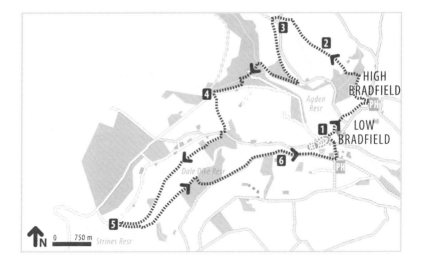

but before the next bridge bear right to enter Windy Bank Wood. Follow the path as it turns left over a bridge and up to a road. Turn right along the road up to a junction and turn left.

4 Join a bridleway soon on the left and follow it to a stile. Bear right downhill through fields, keeping to the left of a wall, to reach Dale Rd. Turn right along the road, soon turning left over a wall stile at the entrance to Dale Dike Reservoir. Follow the track around to the reservoir, continuing ahead along a path on the north side. After a footbridge, take a path over another footbridge, heading uphill on the right to Brogging and Strines Reservoirs.

5 Retrace your steps back to the footbridge, keeping ahead on a path along the southern side of the reservoir. At a fingerpost turn right over a wall stile uphill into a wood, turning left at the next path up to Blindside La. Turn left, keeping ahead as the road descends steadily to Dale Dike at Annet Bridge.

6 Shortly before reaching the bridge, take a path over a stile on the right, continuing ahead across fields and passing cottages until you reach Mill Lee Rd. Turn left downhill into Lower Bradfield. Keep ahead past a bridge on the right and a bus stop to turn right into the car park.

WALK

99 Fox House to Hathersage

START Fox House Inn car park
(free), Hathersage Rd (A6187),
Sheffield, S11 7TY, GR 267803

DISTANCE 9¼ miles (15km)

SUMMARY Moderate, but
rocky uneven paths and a
steep ascent and descent

MAPS OS Explorer OL1 The Peak
District: Dark Peak Area, and
OL24 The Peak District: White
Peak Area; OS Landranger 119

WHERE TO EAT AND DRINK
The Fox House, T01433-
630374, www.vintageinn.co.uk/
thefoxhouselongshaw; Outside Café,
Main Rd, Hathersage, T01433-651936,
www.outside.co.uk/our-stores/
cafe-hathersage.php; National Trust
café, Longshaw T01433-637904

1 From the car park, turn right and follow the A6187 for a couple
of hundred yards before taking the path to the right that passes to the
right of the woods and meets the road at Upper Burbage Bridge.

2 Almost double-back on yourself, but this time pass with the
woods to your left, to reach Higger Tor. Another near-double-back
will take you back to the road; cross it and take the path heading down
to the left. On reaching the road to Hathersage, follow the road briefly
before taking the path past Toothill Farm and then toward Hathersage.

3 Go through a kissing gate on the right and follow the path as it
bears left to emerge through a gate at the back of the church. Turn
right then left through a gate in the churchyard wall. Go ahead, then
right past the cemetery, down to Baulk La. Turn left, then take the
next right (Besom La) to the main road and along to the George
Hotel. Cross the road. Immediately before the Little John public
house, turn right onto a lane. Go under the railway viaduct. At the
gatehouse, the lane bends sharply left. Here, take the field path ahead
to the B6001, close to Leadmill Bridge.

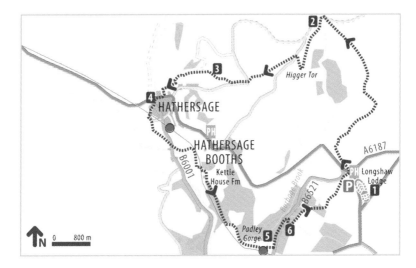

4 Cross the road and follow the lane along the River Derwent to the entrance to Harper Lees. Here, turn left to follow a path as it heads up under the railway and through a gate. Soon, turn right and follow the path (not signed) past Kettle House Farm into woodland. Continue ahead, through a gate, bearing left uphill, and after another gate bear right to a track passing Padley Chapel.

5 Cross the bridge, taking a path over a stile on the left and going straight up Padley Gorge to join a wider path. Turn left on this until it emerges onto the B6521. Go left for a short distance then cross. Immediately turn right onto a narrow path winding through woodland. Continue uphill, keeping left at a fork. Turn left after a gate into more open land, going ahead then bearing right to join a track. Go left, crossing two streams. Soon look out for a less defined track bearing right into trees. Continue ahead to join a path next to a small lake.

6 Turn right onto this path, bearing left to Longshaw. Pass the lodge, keeping left along the access road. Immediately before the gates (onto the B6521), take the path on the right uphill through trees to emerge at Fox House.

100 Hebden Bridge to Withens Clough

START Memorial Gardens,
New Rd (A646), Hebden Bridge,
HX7 8AD, GR 993272

DISTANCE 9½ miles (15.5km)

SUMMARY Moderate; long but
steady climb to Stoodley Pike

MAPS OS Explorer OL21 South
Pennines; OS Landranger 103

WHERE TO EAT AND DRINK Lots
of cafés and pubs in and around
the centre of Hebden Bridge

USEFUL WEBSITE
www.hebdenbridge.co.uk

This walk features a canal towpath, industrial heritage, woodland, moorland and stunning views of the Calder Valley.

① From the Memorial Gardens in the centre of Hebden Bridge cross the canal and turn right to the next bridge. Cross and turn left, following the towpath to Bridge No. 21 carrying the Pennine Way (signposted). Turn left over the bridge onto the Pennine Way and follow the track bearing left uphill through woodland. Keep on the track as it continues uphill, eventually emerging into open farmland to reach a farm at Lower Rough Head.

② After the farm, turn left then immediately right. Follow the field boundary wall, bearing left at the end to a stile. Go left up to a track and fingerpost. Cross and bear right along the Pennine Way, turning right at the next path junction/waymarker for the final ascent to Stoodley Pike.

③ At the Pike turn left and continue on the Pennine Way along the edge until it descends to meet the Calderdale Way at a stone column and waymarker. Turn left onto the Calderdale Way and follow it ahead, turning left at the second gate onto a track heading steadily downhill to reach another track alongside Withens Clough Reservoir. Turn left and follow the track past the reservoir to reach a car park on the right.

④ Turn left onto a lane and follow it uphill on the tarmac surface until it bends sharply left at Stony Royd. Here, turn into the drive

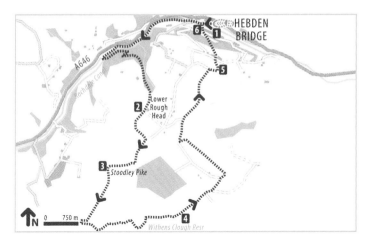

passing the front of the house and through the field beyond to a stile. Go over and turn left along the edge of moorland, following the wall to its end. Turn left to a gate. Do not go through but turn sharp right onto a path, following a wall on the left. Stay on this path, heading gently downhill along the wall. Eventually, at the bottom of a steep descent, with a stile on the left, turn right to a gate on the left. Go through and down through another gate.

⑤   Turn left, keeping ahead on a path following a wall on your right to a stile, bearing right across the next field to a lane. Cross and keep ahead, soon bearing left to a stile in a wall on the left. Follow the path ahead across fields to enter woodland. Continue steeply down through the trees until the path emerges on Park View.

⑥   Cross, turn left and follow the road over the railway. Soon, take the path on the right down steps to the canal. Turn right to reach a bridge over the canal. Retrace your steps to the Memorial Gardens and the start of the walk.

Points of interest

Stoodley Pike Monument was originally completed in 1815 to commemorate the defeat of Napoleon, but it collapsed in 1854. It was rebuilt in 1856 at the end of the Crimean War.

FORTHCOMING TITLES IN THE 100 WALKS SERIES

- Derbyshire
- Wiltshire
- Cheshire
- Northumberland
- Surrey
- Staffordshire
- County Durham

OTHER TITLES IN THE 100 WALKS SERIES

- Lancashire